Hot Topics, Cool Heads

A Handbook for Civil Dialogue

AGREE STRONGLY

AGREE SOMEWHAT

NEUTRAL/ UNDECIDED

DISAGREE SOMEWHAT

DISAGREE STRONGLY

John Genette | Clark D. Olson | Jennifer Linde

Kendall Hunt
publishing company

Cover image © Shutterstock.com

Civil Dialogue®, Hot Topics® and Cool Heads® are US Service Marks registered to the Institute for Civil Dialogue.

Kendall Hunt
publishing company

www.kendallhunt.com
Send all inquiries to:
4050 Westmark Drive
Dubuque, IA 52004-1840

CONTENTS

Foreword v
About the Authors vii

CHAPTER ONE: The Need for Civility 1

CHAPTER TWO: The History and Theory of Civil Dialogue 7

CHAPTER THREE: The Civil Communicator 25

CHAPTER FOUR: Civil Listening 35

CHAPTER FIVE: Creating a Civil Dialogue Event: The Necessary Framework 45

CHAPTER SIX: The Role of the Audience in Civil Dialogue 53

CHAPTER SEVEN: The Art of Facilitation 59

CHAPTER EIGHT: Applications of Civil Dialogue 71

APPENDIX A: Civil Dialogue Placards 81

APPENDIX B: Sample Provocative Statements 99

APPENDIX C: Sample Civil Dialogue Program 103

APPENDIX D: Sample Civil Dialogue Host Introduction 105

APPENDIX E: Sample Civil Dialogue Facilitator Opening Statement 107

APPENDIX F: Sample Civil Dialogue Facilitator Tracking Sheet 111

FOREWORD

Most everyone in society agrees that there is a crying need for civility in our world. From families disagreeing at Thanksgiving tables to the podiums our political leaders speak from, greater civility would be welcomed by all involved. Even controversially appointed Supreme Court Justice Neil Gorsuch remarked on September 28, 2017 from the Trump International Hotel, "To be worthy of our First Amendment freedoms, we have to all adopt certain civil habits that enable others to enjoy them as well. When it comes to the First Amendment, that means tolerate those who don't agree with us or those whose ideas upset us, giving others the benefit of the doubt about their motives."

While it may be popular to talk *about* civility, we have found the people in our communities and classrooms are unable to define civility or even recognize what it looks like. Often people point to recent examples of incivility in their lives and claim that civility must be the opposite. Indeed, most people admit to just avoiding conversations with people with whom they disagree. However, as our discussions ensue, rarely can people put their finger on exactly what civility is, much less know how to practice it.

This is the role Civil Dialogue is designed to play. For nearly 15 years, we have been developing this format as a strategy to give people the tools to understand civility. In this book, we set forth not only a practical definition of civility, but also provide strategies to be used to communicate civilly. We begin with advancing the need for civility, tracing it back to the very roots of democracy. We then articulate how we came to our notion of Civil Dialogue which remains distinct from the numerous other efforts those concerned with civility are teaching. That is followed by a discussion of the skills of a civil communicator with a special focus on civil listening. Chapter Five details the specifics of Civil Dialogue, explaining exactly how to utilize this format. We justify the need for Civil Dialogue to be public, face-to-face, and needing an audience, before we detail the special expertise necessary to successfully facilitate a Civil Dialogue. Finally, we provide numerous applications where we've found Civil Dialogue to be successful, in hopes that our readers might find ways to employ Civil Dialogues in a variety of settings. We also include several appendices which stipulate the specific tools needed to host and facilitate a Civil Dialogue.

Wherever we have taken Civil Dialogue, participants have remarked how valuable it is. Our academic colleagues have found it so successful that the Hugh Downs School of Human Communication has integrated it into the curriculum and even grant a certificate in Civil Communication.

We choose to share our experiences in *Hot Topics, Cool Heads*. Proceeds from this book help fund the Institute for Civil Dialogue (www.civil-dialogue.com) which seeks to host Civil Dialogue events and train facilitators around the country to successfully guide others to communicate civilly. It is our hope that a grassroots awareness of civility will eventually lead to a more civil society.

This book is a product of many people. John wishes to acknowledge Andrea for encouraging his curiosity, professors Linda Park-Fuller and Cheree Carlson for leading him to the body of literature that provided the theoretical framework for Civil Dialogue, and Jennifer and Clark for nurturing, refining, and advancing the concept.

Clark initially thanks John and Jennifer for including him on this journey several years ago. He also thanks Nick for providing him with a full year to write while living abroad. Nick's support, along with the constant companionship of Quincy our Westie and Bernadette our loyal cat, have provided inspiration throughout this project.

Jennifer thanks her Civil Dialogue colleagues John and Clark for many years of interrogating the idea of civility and finding a way to bring civil communication practices to many audiences. She also thanks the many students and community members who have embraced Civil Dialogue as a productive and transformative process.

Collectively, we thank our editor Beth Trowbridge and the publication staff at Kendall Hunt.

ABOUT THE AUTHORS

John Genette is president of Black Mountain Communications Inc. and serves as Civil, Critical & Creative Communication Research Fellow in the Hugh Downs School of Human Communication at Arizona State University. As a graduate student at ASU, he wrote the research paper that set forth the concept of Civil Dialogue. He has presented Civil Dialogue at national conferences and was a founding director of the Institute for Civil Dialogue, serving as its first president.

Clark D. Olson is a professor in the Hugh Downs School of Human Communication at Arizona State University where he has taught for 34 years. He incorporates Civil Dialogue into his argumentation and public speaking classes and has presented Civil Dialogue at conferences nationwide. For 15 years he was the Director of Forensics at ASU, where he coached a nationally successful debate team. From that experience, he articulated the value of Civil Dialogue as distinct from debate, acknowledging a wide variety of opinions instead of arguing polar opposites. He is a founding director of the Institute for Civil Dialogue and currently serves as its president. Clark has published over 40 articles and book chapters and was recognized with the Golden Monograph award in 2005 from the National Communication Association for the best article in the discipline of communication.

Jennifer Linde is a senior lecturer in the Hugh Downs School of Human Communication at Arizona State University, artistic director of The Empty Space (Theatre), and an active member of the I-4C (Civil, Critical, Creative, Communication) research collective at ASU. She engages Civil Dialogue as a pedagogical tool in performance studies classes, has developed courses in civil communication, and facilitated Civil Dialogue events in public and educational contexts since 2004. She has presented Civil Dialogue at national conferences and panels, and is a founding director of the Institute for Civil Dialogue.

CHAPTER ONE:
The Need for Civility

The world is at an apex of disharmony and disagreement. Economic crisis threatens to unravel the Euro zone with respective governments involved vowing a hard-line stance. ISIS troops advance toppling villages and leaving little doubt of their ultimate political and militaristic aims. The possibility of global climate change becomes increasingly evident as weather-related disasters consume various parts of the world. In the United States, Supreme Court decisions are handed down which strike at the very fiber of people's religious and moral beliefs. Public mass shootings seem to occur with regular frequency, and political rivals in Washington threaten inaction on keeping our government funded and working to achieve their own political aims. The recent unexpected election of a polarizing president hardens peoples' political views. Conflict over race relationships at the state and local levels continues to escalate. In fact, never before has such a divide stalled progress among so many intelligent people. What has become obvious on a daily basis is that our world has become *polarized*. According to *New York Times* writer Mark Leibovich, "More and more of us do appear to be locked into our political mind-set" (Leibovich, 2015).

World, national, and local conflict is complex and can often feel overwhelming without the promise of any meaningful solutions. Here is where communication plays a critical role. What is often missing at the core of these disagreements is the shear willingness to sit down and engage in a productive dialogue, listening as well as talking, when confronted with controversial issues. Our nation's leaders are hardly a place to look for models of civility. Politicians, often considering their long game, are reluctant to pause and engage in dialogue for fear of political reprisal or perceived weakness. Even in our presidential campaigns, candidates demean each other with ad hominem attacks such as "nasty, nasty woman," or characterizing one's supporters as a "basket full of deplorables." Is it any wonder that with world leaders so ensconced in their positions that everyday citizens have, likewise, adopted these practices?

Daily news headlines fuel feelings of polarization. Random shooters strike out at a southern church; protesters demonstrating against the removal of Confederate monuments escalate conflicts into riotlike conditions; deranged constituents attack a congresswoman and her staff at a town hall meeting, invade a movie premier, and take aim at an elementary school. Instead of coming together in tragedy, U.S. citizens rage about their Second Amendment right to bear arms and there is an immediate skyrocket in the sale of weapons as people react to the potential of increased regulations on firearms (Baker, 2012). Political candidates seeking offices from the presidency to local mayorship spend millions on negative campaign ads (Edsall, 2012) or conduct last-minute smear campaigns (Wagner & Nanez, 2012), dishing dirt that may be decades old in hopes of gaining a political advantage. Simple attempts of business owners to exercise free speech garner long lines of partisan supporters and threats of violence, and lead to protests and firings of employees who may disagree with the exercise of such rights (Preston, 2012). Even the intended unifying spirit of the Olympics causes excessive nationalism as we applaud loudly for athletes from our own country, while cheering the failures of athletes from other countries.

What has led us, as Americans, to become such a partisan lot? While that question no doubt has hundreds of deeply rooted answers stemming from experiencing terrorist attacks, to increased government regulations intended to protect us, to the explosion of media sources which filter news through admittedly partisan channels, to the advent of social media which allows us to follow and/ or participate in hundreds of opinionated feeds via Facebook, Instagram, Twitter accounts, etc., the end result is that instead of creating productive discourse about the issues of the day, we instead become increasingly polarized in our own opinions. And, the impact of such polarization is that we are able to spend countless hours isolated in front of television and computer screens exposing ourselves to the opinions we already likely hold, rallying other "followers" to take up whatever cause of the day the media spins our way. In the end we must ask ourselves: Toward what goal does this insular opinion sharing aim at achieving? Is it any wonder that our politicians in Washington as well as at local levels are basically gridlocked around party lines, not able to pass simple budgets or pass tax incentives for the good of the country? Or, do we wonder why seasoned politicians refuse to seek reelection, citing the disgust of partisan politics (Steinhauer 2012) fooling ourselves into believing "a return to civility and stability" will follow? (Flake, 2017) Given this vicious cycle, we are left to wonder what our future will be like; instead of holding the optimism of the "American dream" we are shaking our heads at our personal and political inabilities.

Perhaps nowhere is this more obvious than in the simple ability to conduct a conversation with someone who may hold a different opinion than ours. Instead of using our ability to dialogue about issues productively, we instead revel in our partisanship, "unfriending" people with whom we do not see eye to eye politically or religiously, forwarding smoking posts encouraging those we consider friends to "like" our partisan views without really sitting down face to face to have a productive discussion about the root causes or ramifications of certain solutions of specific problems. We have become a society gridlocked by our own partisanship. While it is easiest to blame others for the lack of productive action in today's society, at some point we must take a long, hard look at ourselves and see if our behaviors are not contributing to the problem. Such introspection might just lead to a grass roots movement to restore the "art of conversation" by reintegrating dialogue back into our lives, perhaps even by inviting those with whom we disagree to share in such dialogue to fully examine our own beliefs and why others believe so differently, or have so little interest in the issues we find vitally important.

Much of what passes for dialogue today is inflammatory, sensationalized, and at the very least counterproductive, if not dangerous. Witness South Carolina Representative Joe Wilson's 2010 attack on Barack Obama, when he states, "You lie," during a presidential address to Congress. Television programs like *The McLaughlin Group* and *Hardball* are staged like a shootout at the OK Corral, with pundits and politicians taking verbal shots at each other, interrupting each other and behaving rudely to one another. The word-slinging is apparently good for ratings and revenue, but it has created an atmosphere in which reasoned dialogue with respect for all views is practically nonexistent. *The Christian Science Monitor* in its series "Talking with the Enemy" (2004) emphasized not only the depth of the divide over the 2004 election, but the need to keep talking. As Tannen (2004) noted, people are reluctant to talk because they do not want to have "unseemly arguments." The real problem, she comments, is not knowing how to dialogue across difference. Instead of dialogue, a ritualized opposition or knee-jerk reaction mirrors warlike formats. Such extremism quashes legitimate dissent, creating an inherent sense of imbalance.

Fortunately, we still have a few models of civil communication. On the May 7, 2004, broadcast of "NOW" on PBS, Bill Moyers interviewed Paul Gigot of the *Wall Street Journal*. It was clear that the two men were polar opposites in their political views, but they treated each other civilly. They expressed opposing views (with Moyers's view coming in the form of questions), yet not raising their voices, not getting emotional or seeking to "win" the argument at the cost of advancing the discussion. These two seasoned commentators, however, have the advantage of many years of practice at this sort of dialogue. Many people outside of broadcast journalism also have the *potential* to participate in this type of meaningful and constructive dialogue, but they haven't had an opportunity to practice. Thus, while Moyers and Gigot may not need a facilitator's help to engage in civil dialogue, many of us do.

However, this need for civility is not a new one. Historians point to differences which sparked debate about the creation of the United States, and cite numerous contentious examples from early constitutional debate (Maier, 2010). Even George Washington was credited with creating "Rules of Civility and Decent Behavior" to help guide not only political debate but also social graces. During the same era John Jay at the Constitutional Convention "induced the delegates to treat each others' opinions with tenderness, to argue without asperity, and to endeavor to convince the judgment without hurting the feelings of each other" (Jay, 1888).

Decades ago, commentators identified a breakdown in civility when the U.S. Senate refused to confirm Reagan appointee Robert Bork to the Supreme Court as a turning point in the modern demise of civility on Capitol Hill: "[T]he Bork fight, in some ways, was the beginning of the end of civil discourse in politics" (Nocera, 2011). The rift over the 2000 election of President George W. Bush essentially decided by the Supreme Court along party lines and the subsequent rancor over the response to invade Iraq post 9-11, coupled with Bush's controversial reelection campaign in 2004, has raised a new awareness for the need for civility in Washington. Was American democracy created so the will of the majority rule can be replaced with the ugly partisanship we witness today?

Yet, it is not only on a national or governmental level where the need for civility arises. We take ourselves as an example. On January 1, 2012, the *Arizona Republic* ran as their headline article a story on civility and the current lack of civility which surrounded the Tucson Tragedy and subsequent attempts to foster civility in Arizona. The article quoted us and our efforts to encourage civility, including hosting Accessing Civility: Arizona Forum on Civil Communication in February (McKinnon, 2012). However, the responding comments via online posts regarding efforts toward civility were "uncivil" at best. Hitman commented, "The hypocrisy of the writers and editors of this paper never, ever ceases to amaze me. How ironic is it that an article decrying political 'uncivility' appears in a paper that does everything it can to tweak the majority and attempt to affect social change with it's [sic] obvious bias and other dirty little tricks?" Hickory Hill echoed this comment with one of his/her own: "Unfortunately the liberal-leftist machinations claim they want civility when in actuality all they want is their way. How can one be civil when the liberals want to unhinge this country? Those of us for public safety and peace in our country are always considered to be freaks." The article was even derided on a national level when it was picked up by *USA Today* ("After Giffords shooting," 2012). Jenny Zora commented, "Civility in this country is dead . . . both sides are to blame for it." Mary Cunningham shared her frustration, "Civil Discourse? We can't even seem to have it on this post, why think it might be possible in the wake of this horrible event? The ugliness is palpable. Instead of embracing the changing face of America, disdain and anger grew. Finger pointing, innuendo and accusations, name calling and blame assessing have mushroomed." Larry Bennatt was perhaps most damning when he wrote, "Ridiculous piece of drivel." Such comments surrounding the issue of civility point to the overwhelming need for citizens to practice civility.

While disciplines such as sociology (Hall, 2013) and political science (Geer, 2006; Strachan & Wolf, 2010) have decried the current lack of civility, civility is perhaps nowhere more appropriate than for scholars of communication. As early as 1989, Krippendorff commented, "Dialogue probably is the most noble form of human interaction, and communication scholars should be the first to appreciate its outstanding human qualities" (p. 94). Toward this aim, we focus on the creation of "Civil Dialogue." As we will explain in the following chapter, many attempts have been made to use dialogue toward various political ends. And the notion of civility has received some slight treatment, usually when discussing "incivility," which we note is much easier to do as examples are rife. We contend that civility is not merely the opposite or absence of incivility, but includes numerous properties which can be practiced toward a mutually beneficial end.

Despite current practice and claims that civility is dead, we propose a format to encourage civility—a format that can be used to discuss "Hot Topics with Cool Heads." That format is Civil Dialogue. Throughout the past decade, Civil Dialogue has been developed, modified, and evolved; it has been tapped by political, community, and educational leaders across the country and abroad as a way to conduct civil conversations among people who may disagree across a spectrum of opinions. As the scholars who've researched, taught, and practiced civil dialogues on countless controversial issues, we invite you to consider how you might use Civil Dialogue in your communities, churches, classrooms; in your research; or in contemporary practice. As can be widely seen, politicians may greatly benefit from such a format, as community leaders are desperate to help constituencies make better policies.

Even the most basic social group, the family, has difficulty talking about issues, whether it be a highly charged political or social issue, simple plans for a family vacation, or an emotionally laden issue like planning a funeral for a parent or loved one. Whatever the context, we encourage you to investigate what we've learned about Civil Dialogue and about how it has changed the way we view the world. Perhaps starting at a grass roots level, by learning such skills in a classroom or workshop, then like a pebble causing a ripple in a pool, others will witness your civility and may want to become involved. Once local issues become discussed passionately and respectfully, and participants and audience members witness that it is possible to have disagreements without the express goal of conversion or persuasion, but to achieve some mutual level of understanding, then other decision makers at higher levels will recognize and pursue participation in dialogues which are civil, earnestly seeking to learn about areas of disagreements. Perhaps the largest jump occurs when our politicians actually start practicing the art of Civil Dialogue.

Civil Dialogue is working to instruct citizens of all cultures, groups, political parties, religions, generations, and belief systems that it is possible to sit down and cogently share ideas of disagreement, express themselves passionately, while really working to understand why those who hold differing, perhaps even opposite opinions may well be as deeply convicted as themselves. This is the express goal of Civil Dialogue and the one that through a theoretical explanation, outlining some practical steps, elucidating some communication skills that we all too frequently forget, and then learning of different forums for practicing Civil Dialogue can we ever hope, first to change the vicious polarizations within ourselves, and then work toward productively engaging in dialogues with those with whom we disagree. Once we can model this skill, our feelings toward each other are likely to warm and we may find ways to actually work together to achieve a better world, instead of just pessimistically claiming the one we live in is doomed.

The answer may be as simple as Civil Dialogue explained in these next few chapters to help you, and groups you are affiliated with, to be able to engage in civility.

REFERENCES

Baker, M. (2012). Gun sales spike after shooting. *The Arizona Republic* (July 26): A1, A9.

Edsall, T. B. (2012). The politics of anything goes. *The New York Times* (July 23).

Finnerty, M. (2012). Despite spoilers, we're still watching London Olympics. *The Arizona Republic* (August 1): D1.

Flake, J. (2017). Mr. President, I rise today to say: Enough. *The Arizona Republic* (October 25): A1, 17.

Geer, J. J. (2006). *In defense of negativity: Attack ads in presidential campaigns.* Chicago: University of Chicago Press.

Hall, J. A. (2013). *The importance of being civil.* Princeton, NJ: Princeton University Press.

Hamilton, A., Jay, J., & Madison, J. (1888). The Federalist : a commentary on the Constitution of the United States being a collection of essays written in support of the Constitution agreed upon September 17, 1787, by the Federal convention. Lodge, H. C. (Ed.). New York: G. P. Putnam's Sons.

Krippendorf, K. (1989). On the ethics of constructing communication. In Dervin, B., Grossberg, L., O'Keefe, J. J., & Wartella, E. (Eds.), *Rethinking communication: Vol 1*:66-96. Newberry Park, CA: Sage.

Leibovich, Mark. (2015). Divided we stand. *The New York Times Magazine* (April 12): 13–15.

Maier, P. (2010). *Ratification: The people debate the Constitution, 1787-1788.* New York, NY: Simon & Schuster.

McKinnon, S. (2012). After shooting near Tucson, civil discourse still elusive. *The Arizona Republic* (January 1): A1

Nocera, J. (2011). The ugliness started with Bork. *The New York Times* (October 22): A15.

Preston, J. (2012). Chick-fil-A draws huge crowds for appreciation day. *The New York Times* (August 1): A1.

Preston, J., Brown, R., & Severson, K. (2012). Gay couples head to Chick-fil-A for kiss-in protest. *The New York Times* (August 3): A1.

Steinhauer, J. (2012). Olympia Snowe won't seek re-election. *The New York Times* (February 28): A1.

Strachan, J. C., & Wolf, M. R. (2012). Political civility: Introduction to political civility. *Political Science & Politics 45*: 401-404.

Talking with the enemy: A series to help Americans bridge the bittered-blue divide. (2004). *Christian Science Monitor.* Retrieved from http://www.csmonitor.com/2004/1022/p09s01-coop.html

Tannen, D. (2004). We need high quality outrage. *Christian Science Monitor* (October 22): 9.

Wagner, D., & Nanez, D. M. (2012). Mark Mitchell cries foul over 1983 abuse allegation. *The Arizona Republic* (May 1): B1.

CHAPTER TWO:
The History and Theory of Civil Dialogue

C ivil Dialogue (a.k.a. "Hot Topics, Cool Heads") features spontaneous, face-to-face inter-action among citizens/students (not a panel of experts) in an atmosphere that promotes respect and equanimity. A trained facilitator introduces audience members to consider a provocative statement, and volunteer participants are called upon to embody their positions in a semicircle of five chairs on stage — "Agree Strongly," "Agree Somewhat," "Neutral/Undecid-ed," "Disagree Somewhat," and "Disagree Strongly." It is not a contest; the goal is not to seek ad-vocacy but to reacquaint the public with the notion that citizens can have differing viewpoints or disagree without demonizing the opposition. Participants are invited to give opening state-ments, followed by a guided but spontaneous discussion of their viewpoints; audience members are solicited for their questions and input; participants make closing statements; and the round of dialogue concludes with the facilitator's summary.

WHAT IS CIVILITY?

Initially, it is necessary to define what the nature of civility is, and also to assess what it is not. To us, civility means authentically sharing one's feelings and basis for making value judgments on socially important issues. It is honestly providing insights into one's moral code in a setting of respectfulness. As such, it is not free from the judgement of others, but demonstrates a willing-ness to put one's thoughts into the public arena for scrutiny. We take exception with philosopher Cheshire Calhoun (2000) who equates civility with etiquette and a certain amount of politeness (i.e., being respectful, considerate, and tolerant). Calhoun suggests that "civility forestalls the potential unpleasantness of a life with other people" (p. 251). We couldn't disagree more. Our world today is filled with unpleasantness and with people who deeply hold beliefs and philosophical positions contrary to our own. In a civil society, we contend one does not withhold these personal beliefs merely to avoid the potential of offending another. To do so would only be to stifle one's deep-seated values. We agree with Rawls (1971) who writes that civility requires that people be "willing to explain the grounds of their actions" (p. 179). We argue that civilly revealing one's values, whatever they are, and however they were formed, is essential to a democratic society. In legal scholar Stephen Carter's (1998, 2011) words, "it has nothing to do with people being nice to each other." Instead, civil citizens actually risk offending one another toward a greater goal of being understood.

Obviously, any democracy is comprised of a variety of contradictory viewpoints, and consensus is rarely, if ever, reached on such deep-seated issues as race, religion, sex, security, etc. Instead, there exists an ever-present tension where policies change and develop to suit the needs of the time. Restraining speech only forestalls this evolutionary process for the sake of niceness. We contend that civility must exist even, and especially, in the face of grave disagreements. Calhoun (2000) assumes, "All agree that civility is, importantly, a matter of restraining speech" (p. 257). We, respectfully, disagree. It is using one's voice, not restraining it, that is essential to democracy. Whereas Calhoun provides a political concept of civility as "what fits us for life in a pluralistic society, wherein nonlike-minded people will have to enter into political dialogue in order to reach compromise agreements" (p. 269); we doubt that agreement is ever reached. Instead, merely revealing the nature and act of disagreement comprises an important step in civility. Indeed, in quoting etiquette expert Miss Manners, Calhoun questions when the "bounds of civility" have been reached. In equating civility with morality and the embodiment of a moral framework, we hold that limiting people to a certain bounds of acceptability standard will only serve to strengthen their viewpoints which likely need to be challenged.

Calhoun (2000) further contends that "civility is owed only to people who have (in one's best judgement) gotten it more or less right. People one judges to have gotten hold a morally pernicious view are not owed a civil response" (p. 271). As such, Calhoun limits civility to only those who share our opinions and viewpoints, attitudes, and beliefs. Calhoun concludes that "civility is a virtue that we are required to exercise toward others only if they pursue *socially* acceptable views and behaviors" (p. 272). In today's political climate, the paucity of civility demonstrated by our national leaders would only increase if this standard was upheld.

Conversely, we argue that what is socially acceptable is constantly in a state of flux and negotiation, with agreement unlikely to be reached. As such, extremist views, particularly ones contrary to our own, are fundamentally necessary to discuss with an air of freedom and unrestraint. It is through the investigation of points of disagreement we are able to pursue democracy. Only when Donald Trump's beliefs that all Muslims are potential terrorists or Kim Davis's contention that all gays and lesbians who seek marriage rights are morally repugnant—positions on which a number of the citizenry concur—are placed in a forum to dissect the deep-seated rationales for these beliefs, can civility ever hope to be achieved. Instead of jeering at opinions with which we disagree, listening to the likely reasons behind these beliefs can aid us in ultimately learning about the roots of such disagreements. Being able to reveal, probe, and discuss such values is what we argue constitutes real civility and our efforts at doing so embody a civil citizenry. Contrary to what Gutmann and Thompson (1990) suggest, that "a civil citizen simply seeks for points of moral agreement" or Kingwell (1995) who notes that civility requires a "willingness not to say all the true, or morally excellent things one could say" (p. 211) we believe one cannot limit civility to merely those with whom we agree. Civility exists in embracing disagreement, not in pursuing agreement. Indeed, we would equate cowardice with politeness. Not expressing one's viewpoint for fear of disagreement is the antithesis of civility, not the embodiment of it. The key to civility becomes how to achieve this aim.

WHAT IS DIALOGUE?

In its simplest form, a dialogue is a conversation; however, it is much more than just "talk." In his seminal book *On Dialogue,* David Bohm (1996) provides the pivotal definition that "dialogue is aimed at the understanding of consciousness" (p. xx). This stands to reason if one looks at the etymology of the word *dialogue,* which derives from the Greek word *dialogos. Logos* means "the word," and *dia* means "through" (Bohm, 1996, p. 6). Civil Dialogue is not restricted to two opposing viewpoints, but seeks a range of interpretations to create conscious meaning.

Dialogue begins as people start to discuss an issue, something on which there is not general agreement, but wherein controversy exists. Bohm (1996) notes that dialogue best occurs in a place where there is no authority, hierarchy, special purpose, or agenda, in essence an "empty place" where anything can be talked about (p. 49). Despite advances in technology and the greater access to vast communication channels, he restricts dialogue to face-to-face encounters so that none of the communication message is lost in translation. Dialogue provides an opportunity for people to share strong feelings which can bring about strong emotional responses. While it may begin by focusing on the entire thought process, the end result is often to see something of each other's humanity. In that, Neisser and Hess (2012, p. 188) concur with us that dialogue brings about better understanding. It is the opportunity to learn first hand what another believes and, more importantly, why. Dialogue seems to harness "collective intelligence" of the people around us, so that we all become more aware and more intelligent as individuals (Isaacs, 1999, p. 11). As President Obama has suggested, "Challenging each other's ideas can renew our democracy. But when we challenge each other's motives, it becomes harder to see what we hold in common" (Fletcher, 2010).

As such, in Civil Dialogue there is no final decision required of anyone. Without decisions, there are no winners and losers; there is no such thing as being right. People can express an opinion and feel free to change their minds just as readily as they may be more convinced of their original conviction. It allows disagreement without hostility and can make conflict productive (Hall, 2013, p. 4). In a "civil" dialogue, everybody "shows respect for" everybody (Cuddihy, 1978). The key question is just *how* to accomplish this.

CIVIL DIALOGUE IS GROUNDED IN RHETORICAL AND PERFORMANCE THEORY

The notion of civility has long been considered by scholars in various disciplines. Anderson (2011) has provided a historical look at race and civility. Alexander (2006) has written a sociological viewpoint of civility, while Hall (2013) provides various political philosophies and the relative impact of those philosophies on civility. Our approach differs in that our notion of Civil Dialogue is anchored in the discipline of communication.

Inspired by Augusto Boal's (1995) interactive Theatre of the Oppressed, Forum Theatre, and Legislative Theatre, Walter Ong's (2000) notion that "thought is nested in speech," and Denzin's (2003) call for nurturing "critical democratic imagination," Civil Dialogue is grounded in both rhetorical and performance theory. The driving force behind the development of Civil Dialogue in 2004 was the desire to create a forum in which citizens could examine the persuasive impact of political speeches. The need for such a forum was evident and urgent. The United States had invaded Iraq, political candidates were deeply divided about the wisdom of that military action, and ordinary citizens were unable to conduct even-tempered conversations about such a heated and controversial topic. Indeed, Yankelovich (2004) observed in *The Christian Science Monitor* that "seemingly irreconcilable differences" had "split the nation down the middle," with friendly dinner parties devolving to "clenched teeth" when the conversation turned to politics. As David Brooks (2010) of the *New York Times* would later observe, we were living in a country "in which many people live in information cocoons in which they only talk to members of their own party and read blogs of their own sect."

The influence of rhetorical theory is evident in Crowley (1992), who issued a call to action:

> To the extent that ordinary citizens are unable to articulate or criticize the discursive conditions that cause and maintain unfair and destructive practices, we academic rhetoricians must bear some responsibility for their silence. Our retreat into philosophical idealism and our concern with technique have reduced us to bickering

among ourselves when what we ought to be doing, rather, is showing people how rhetoric is practiced, how language is deployed as a means of coercion, and how they can resist that coercion (464).

 Crowley stopped short, however, of laying out a specific *plan* for showing people how rhetoric is practiced. Civil Dialogue is an effort to fill that gap, informed by the work of performance practitioners such as Boal (1995). Carlson (1999) explains that, for Boal, "art merged with daily activity" as "a means of exploring social situations and of developing leadership and coping skills in the participant/audience" (p. 120). Jackson (2004) explains that Boal developed the Legislative Theatre as "a way of using theatre within a political system to produce a truer form of democracy" (p. xviii). One of Boal's (1995) most important concepts is the notion of balance, or protecting the forum itself from being overrun by one polarized view, and this tenet is foundational for Civil Dialogue, exemplified by the full range of possible viewpoints—from Agree Strongly to Disagree Strongly—being represented in each round of Civil Dialogue regardless of whether the equal distribution of time to each viewpoint is reflective of the spectrum of viewpoints in the audience. Jackson (2004) reminds us that Boal's Forum Theatre

> [w]as never about a simplification into right and wrong, never in absolute terms of black and white—one person's black might be another person's white, or grey, or red, or blue or yellow, or whatever. . . . Forum never seeks to impose any kind of doctrine of political correctness, nor to make things easy; easier to understand, maybe (p. xix).

Boal's effort to achieve balance is similar to the problem-solving model articulated by Watzlawick, Weakland, and Fisch (1974). As a metaphor for the manner in which people attempt to solve conflict in interpersonal communication, they imagine two sailors "hanging out of either side of a sail boat in order to steady it," noting that the more one of the sailors leans overboard, the more the other "has to hang out to compensate for the instability created by the other's attempt to stabilize the boat, while the boat itself would be quite steady if not for their acrobatic efforts at steadying it" (p. 36). Steadying the boat in Civil Dialogue is the job of the facilitator, the role that Boal describes as the "joker," master of ceremonies, conductor, improvisational coach, teacher, and entertainer rolled into one essential player. If the dialogue is dominated by one extreme position or the other, the event could disintegrate into a partisan screed and alienate not only the opposition but also the undecided. Civil Dialogue events do not intend to lean too much to one side or the other. Rather, the facilitator should keep the boat steady by inviting counterweight to extreme views. Only by insisting on balance can Civil Dialogue ever be useful to the broad community.

CIVIL DIALOGUE IS DESIGNED TO ENCOURAGE SPEECH

In order for the public to participate in dialogue in an articulate manner, Ong (2000) reminds us that verbalizing is necessary because "thought is nested in speech" (p. 138). "In all human cultures," Ong explains, "the spoken word appears as the closest sensory equivalent of fully developed interior thought" (p. 138). Further, Ong argues that true communication requires the "public presence" of one person with another. When we contact one another via electronic means, Ong posits, we are not communicating in the purest sense because electronic mediums create an "artificial oral-aural public presence" (p. 15). In short, the format of Civil Dialogue supports the idea that face-to-face is better than Facebook or other forms of computer-mediated communication.

Portelli (1994) argues that orality is "the primary phenomenon of human life" but has been displaced by the act of writing. In his view, however, writing doesn't have to replace or abolish orality: "The advantage of our literate (and electronic) cultures over exclusively oral ones does not lie in the fact that we possess better tools of communication but that we possess more of them, alongside one another" (p. 5). The human voice, Portelli argues, is "materially accessible to all," while an individual's use of other technologies can be restricted. "With the advent of writing, we no longer relate to others in terms of concrete, direct, mutual understanding but increasingly depend on mediated, written reconstructions" (p. 6).

Chanan (1995) argues that the advent of broadcast technology, radio and television, made things even worse, transforming the masses from active oral creatures to passive listeners and degrading what we understand as political deliberation into "*virtual* deliberation" (p. 120; emphasis added). Hague and Loader (1999) agree, observing that our dependence on media has discouraged critical thinking, as "citizens watch and listen to the elite thinking aloud on behalf of the public" (p. 196).

If Ong (2000) is correct, that clarity of thought is linked to speaking words, and if Hague and Loader (1999) are correct, that we are no longer thinking aloud for ourselves, then we need to find ways to reverse the trend and restore a balance between speaking and listening. We listen to speech blasting from our car radios, we listen to speech in movie theatres and on television, but as a society we are frequently not engaged in a meaningful response to what we hear, thus we are not gaining the maximum benefit of our oral nature. Especially in the midst of elections, when hot topics are hottest and we are inundated with campaign ads, we would be wise to heed Burke's (1940) reminder that political rhetoric can be powerfully coercive, citing Hitler's ability to swing "a great people into his wake" (p. 2). (We do not portend that American politicians share Hitler's sinister nature, only that the intent to persuade is inherent in politics, and that a mastery of coercion is fundamental to success in politics.) We answer Crowley's (1992) call to action by taking time to reflect upon this rhetoric in the manner that Ong suggests gets us closest to clarity of thought: by speaking our minds.

Who better to lead an oral revival than the rhetoricians who already revere the spoken word and the practice of speaking? Perhaps it is indeed time, as Crowley (1992) says, to "accept our professional responsibility to the communities in which we live" (p. 464). If we do not help our communities engage in the issues of our time, we may render rhetorical practice moot.

Throughout the remainder of this essay, we contrast Civil Dialogue with the format of academic debate, acknowledge past theories which have attempted to incorporate aspects of civility, and then look to other formats of dialogue which have developed to fill this need, while noting the uniqueness of the Civil Dialogue format to promote articulation and understanding of divergent positions on "hot topics" while keeping "cool heads."

DIALOGUE VS. DEBATE

In both theory and practice, Civil Dialogue is distinct from debate as we have come to know it today. We compare and contrast the two formats here to shed light on the distinctions between them, and to confirm the unique contribution Civil Dialogue makes to the "toolbox" of techniques, approaches, and formats available to promoters of civility.

Most training in today's argument-driven culture focuses on competition. Typically, debate has the goal of advocacy. The concept of debate in nearly all formats (i.e., traditional, parliamentary, Oxford, Lincoln-Douglas, etc.) is predicated on a decision, rendered either by a judge or judges or the audience. At the central core of debate is the goal of decision making, with the debaters advocating opposing viewpoints on differing sides of a resolution. At typical tournaments, debaters alternate sides to demonstrate their ability to advocate both sides of a position, but each round of debate typically ends with a judge casting a decision in favor of one side or the other, declaring a specific winner and loser based on a certain set of criteria, depending on the style of debate. Contrastingly, Civil Dialogue has as its core mission seeking understanding of the issues surrounding the "hot topic." Whereas debate may well increase the understanding of participants, that education is the by-product of the debate. By presenting a full spectrum of opinions on an issue from "Agree Strongly" to "Disagree Strongly," Civil Dialogue seeks to increase the understanding of why people believe the positions that they take. Involving the audience furthers this aim by allowing additional active participation that is not limited by an obligation to render a final decision. As such, Civil Dialogue focuses more on the process than does debate. Debate focuses predominantly on the outcome of the interaction whereas Civil Dialogue focuses on the process of initiating understanding. A final decision in Civil Dialogue is immaterial and, in fact, never even called for. There are no declared winners or losers, as it is the aim that everyone leaves with a greater understanding of viewpoints, particularly those which are most polarized.

Secondly, debate is traditionally based on evidence. Many a debater has spent countless hours researching opposing viewpoints, culling through thousands of articles, opinions, studies, and testimonies. In the decision-making process, many a judge has likewise called for crucial pieces of evidence to weigh their merits on such evidentiary standards as methodology, recency, and/or credibility before casting a decision. Civil Dialogue does not depend on evidence, but is predicated upon the existing knowledge and viewpoints of the participants. Certainly a well-informed citizenry is essential to a thought-provoking dialogue, but realistically, not all citizens are well informed. In this respect, Civil Dialogue mirrors real life. Other than age and residency restrictions, nearly every adult, save convicted felons, is eligible to vote in most elections. The outcome of most elections often hinges on those with only a passing knowledge of issues and often is determined by those voters who are undecided prior to an election, those who mirror the "neutral" or "undecided" position in a Civil Dialogue. As such, much of the decision making around electing governmental representatives, federal, state, and local, as well as state and local referenda are determined by people's existing knowledge. A core goal of Civil Dialogue is to allow citizens to voice their positions from an experiential position rather than a researched position.

The final distinction between debate and Civil Dialogue is in the nature of polarizing differences. In debate, participants must advocate one position or the other as they represent affirmative/negative or government/opposition sides. Most of the time, other than during winning coin flips in elimination rounds, debaters have no say over which side they represent. And in most tournament formats, they will have the opportunity to represent both sides approximately equally. In order to invest in their positions, debaters often take extreme positions, highlighting opposition and maximizing clash. Indeed, debate is predicated on contested issues (Freeley & Steinberg, 2009). As debaters work to strategically win debates, they will often invest in positions extreme in nature, highlighting the very differences between affirmative and negative ground. Many a successful debater can advocate equally well for both sides. While successful debaters are able to acknowledge which portions of arguments they can lose without losing a round of debate, the very activity rewards those who advocate successfully for one side or the other. Indeed, most debate ballots force this polarizing distinction by forcing the judge to determine "the better debating was done by the affirmative or negative side" in the debate.

Civil Dialogue does not make such a distinction. Indeed, by its very format, it allows, even encourages neutrality on an issue. It supports indecision and throughout the process, not only allows for a middle ground between polarizing viewpoints (the "Agree" and "Disagree" positions are joined by "Neutral" or "Undecided"), but even permits participants to change their mind during the dialogue. The facilitator frequently asks as a dialogue is ending if anyone would switch seats or if people have felt any movement in their position during the dialogue. Indeed, while it is rare to have those firmly entrenched in their positions alter their viewpoints, often the three middle seats admit some fluctuation in their viewpoints, either stronger toward the side which they originally took, or sometimes drifting toward the middle to a state of neutrality, to occasionally moving across the aisle, so to speak, to believe a position contrary to the one they originally took. Since there is no winner or loser in a Civil Dialogue, such movement is acknowledged, and even encouraged.

OTHER THEORETICAL PERSPECTIVES

It is useful to consider Civil Dialogue in comparison to Foss and Griffin's (1995) invitational rhetoric in that they both share self-determination, allowing individuals to make their own decisions about how they wish to live their lives (p. 4). Toward this end, Civil Dialogue and invitational rhetoric share the "invitation to the audience to enter the rhetor's world and to see it as the rhetor does . . . trying to understand the rhetor's perspective and then presenting their own . . . so that everyone involved gains a greater understanding of the issue in its subtlety, richness, and complexity" (p. 5). However, Civil Dialogue is not predicated on the need to create relationships in that most dialogues typically only span 45 minutes, hardly time for a relationship formation with likely strangers from the public.

Furthermore, Foss and Griffin (1995) contend that given the openness of invitational rhetoric, resistance is not anticipated. Given the provocative nature of Civil Dialogue with the full range of opinions from Strongly Agree to Strongly Disagree, participants will share multiple, often inconsistent perspectives or worldviews that any single rhetor could perceive as resistant to his/her viewpoints. The spontaneous nature of Civil Dialogue often does not permit the time necessary to identify "possible impediments to understanding," as invitation rhetoric calls for. With mutual understanding as the stated goal, it is not incumbent on speakers to reason why certain people who disagree might do so. As a result, unlike in invitational rhetoric, Civil Dialogue participants don't "seek to minimize or neutralize [impediments]" (p. 5).

Foss and Griffin (1995) postulate three external conditions are necessary for invitational rhetoric: safety, value, and freedom. Civil Dialogue does not attempt to achieve any of these aims. Initially, while Civil Dialogue seeks to create a supportive environment for all viewpoints, we recognize that we cannot guarantee safely, in that safety requires security and freedom from danger. Civil Dialogues exist in public forums with no prescreening for opinions. While our attempt to be supportive is sincere, we have no control over the viewpoints, opinions, and narratives shared, and indeed have encountered situations in which all participants may not be secure in their feeling of safety, in that what constitutes safety differs radically from person to person based on past experiences. We cannot censor what Civil Dialogue participants share. While invitational rhetoric's safety condition specifies that audience members do not fear rebuttal, given the full span of opinions necessary for a Civil Dialogue, there is often rebuttal as peoples' world experiences and viewpoints differ greatly.

Secondly, Foss and Griffin (1995) define the notion of "value" as not only listening "carefully to the perspectives of others but try[ing] to think from those perspectives" (p. 12). Civil Dialogue does not encourage participants to think from the perspective of another, merely to clearly state their own worldview. Indeed, we would contend that given some peoples' life experiences, their opinions are so entrenched that it is not possible to step outside one's own standpoint.

Finally, "freedom" in invitational rhetoric allows others to accept or reject the perspectives of other rhetors, connoting that a rhetor "is not offended, disappointed, or angry if audience members choose not to adopt a particular perspective" (p. 12). We acknowledge that in Civil Dialogue, we cannot control the emotions of a participant and indeed the possibility exists for them to feel offended, disappointed, and angry given the potential responses in a dialogue. Civil Dialogue is meant to be provocative, and that provocation may spur emotional responses that are inconsistent with the freedom external condition of invitational rhetoric.

In responding to the multiplicity of critiques offered of invitational rhetoric, one of the original architects of the theory even links invitational rhetoric to civility (Bone, Griffin, & Scholz, 2008). However, as developed, invitational rhetoric is only "a move toward civility" (p. 456), as the authors separate their invitational approach by merely adding the term "civility." They contend that their examples "suggest that when we adopt an invitational approach *and* are civil, the potential for grief and violence is minimized" (p. 456). Furthermore, they "suggest that civility, *and* invitational rhetoric can be understood as an approach to communication and an integral component of democracy" (p. 457; italics added). They make no attempt to conflate civility with invitational rhetoric or explain how invitational rhetoric is essential to achieving civility, merely that they "speak from a place of invitation, of civility" (p. 457). As one specific critique notes, invitational rhetoric is premised on the notion of power equality, assuming "shared interests between oppressors and oppressed, so that conflict may be ostensibly be solved through mutual invitation" (Lozano-Reich & Cloud, 2009, p. 221). However, Lozano-Reich and Cloud continue to note that "the powerful rarely are willing to invite those less powerful into dialogue; the oppressed are hard pressed to convince oppressors who benefit materially from oppression to be open to dialogue, let alone radical change" (p. 222). This inequity has called them to encourage action through incivility. In contrast to this critique of invitational rhetoric, we posit that given the public notion of Civil Dialogue, that all strata of power are "invited" to dialogue. We have witnessed politicians engaged in Civil Dialogues with constituents, national elders of a church in Civil Dialogue with the youth of the same denomination. Civil Dialogue provides the egalitarian invitation and puts all voices on an equal playing field in an effort to model and promote civility.

Another theory of the use of dialogue is in political and dialogic deliberation (Kim & Kim, 2008). They consider two dimensions of deliberative democracy, instrumental deliberation (a procedural tool through which people negotiate and make decisions) and dialogic, through which people construct the concept of the self and other (p. 51). In their analysis of dialogic deliberation, they contend that the free interaction of others to enhance mutual and self-understanding results "in the production and reproduction of rules, shared values, and public reasons for deliberation" (p. 53). Clearly, Civil Dialogue is distinct from dialogic deliberation in that spontaneous political conversations do occur within an already established framework of rules to ensure fairness to all positions in the dialogue. For Kim and Kim (2008) political talk must be carried out "without being constrained by formal procedural rules and predetermined agenda" (p. 53). In their discussion of everyday political talk they suggest that "(a) people do not have preformed opinions, but rather multiple and often conflicting opinion elements about an issue; (b) people usually do not realize that they have conflicting opinion elements until they have had a chance to discuss and reflect on their thoughts about an issue; and (c) only when people have had an opportunity to express their opinions by speaking do they try to organize their opinions in more coherent ways—consistent with what they 'say' and what they now believe" (p. 61). While it has been our experience that occasionally some people find themselves holding contradictory ideas, we offer the neutral or undecided position for these discussants to work through their viewpoints. Ultimately, Kim and Kim conclude that both instrumentation and dialogic deliberation are necessary for the goal of democracy, as "we can collectively negotiate to achieve a consensus" (p. 66). Again, while Civil Dialogue may embody certain elements of dialogic deliberation, its ultimate goal is not to achieve the democratic goal of consensus.

Another tact in the discussion of dialogue as public deliberation (Heidelbaugh, 2008), predicated on rhetorical theory, views dialogue as "constantly negotiating several inherent tensions" (p. 29). As such, according to Hammond, Anderson, and Cissna (2003) "the process of dialogue in some sense becomes its own goal" (p. 138). Heidelbaugh discusses openness and cooperativeness as essential criteria for dialogue, with a need for change in participants' relationship. In Civil Dialogue, however, the goal is not change, but is to itself model civility; hence, its goal rests not in the outcome of the dialogue, but is a pre-outcome-based format where the outcome of civility is recognized and practiced in the process itself.

Without addressing the concept of dialogue itself, Iris Young (2000) makes a threefold argument for what is essential for inclusive political communication: greeting, rhetoric, and narrative. Greeting, she writes, is "prior to and a condition for making assertions and giving reasons for them, is a moment of opening to and directly acknowledging the other" (p. 58). It involves the risk of trusting others to sustain a discussion of the issues at hand. "Rhetoric are the ways that political assertions and arguments are expressed" (p. 53). Narrative, which frequently occurs in Civil Dialogues, "empowers relatively disfranchised groups to assert themselves publicly; it also offers means by which people whose experiences and beliefs differ so much that they do not share enough premises to engage in fruitful debate can nevertheless reach dialogical understanding" (p. 53). Young expands the concept of the narrative by concluding: "Stories often serve as the only means for people in one social segment to gain some understanding of experiences, needs, projects, problems, and pleasures of people in the society differently situated from themselves" (p. 74). Without invoking the either the term *civil* or *dialogue*, Young comes closest to identifying the power we witness in the practice of Civil Dialogue. It allows minority opinions to be voiced, supports the rhetorical choices they make in this voicing, and allows a strong place for narrative, which we believe is a strong foundation on which people base their opinions and beliefs.

OTHER FORMATS

Not surprisingly, we are not the first to recognize the growing need for ways to promote dialogue and public deliberation in a democratic society. Since 2002 the National Coalition for Dialogue and Deliberation (www.ncdd.org) has served as a clearinghouse for the many and varied resources and formats that are commonly used toward this aim. This section will review several of the more popular formats in which dialogue is used and identify key differences with the Civil Dialogue format.

One of the earliest efforts grew from an awareness of the low level of civic literacy. In 1981 the National Issues Forum (formalized in 1989; www.nifi.org) began to seek citizen involvement in the political process. Using a town meeting format, which today includes online forums, NIF is predicated on the wisdom that citizens have that which is not known by experts. As participants "stew and mull over options" they work to enhance "citizen understanding" of the issues within a democracy. They claim to embody deliberative democracy with seven elements: "*Actors* make *choices* by *deliberative dialogue* to come to *public judgment* and thereby establish a *public voice* through *common ground* and *complementary action*" (Pearce & Littlejohn, 1997, p. 173). They offer extensive preparation in the form of videos and issue booklets to inform the public. Pearce and Littlejohn claim: "The heart of deliberation is consideration of the actual choices" (p. 176). The ultimate focus is on the decision, "Citizens cannot act together until they decide together" (NIF Overview). The NIF typically focuses on a single major issue per year, and hosts large gatherings throughout the nation on this issue.

Obviously Civil Dialogue is predicated on the knowledge of ordinary citizens as well. However, there is the clear absence of choice and there is no need for a final decision. Civil Dialogues typically are shorter, and participants bring to the process their own knowledge and experiences, no advanced preparations are necessary, and typically only the general topic area is announced, so there are not partisan speakers advocating for a particular position.

Following closely on the heels of NIF, the Public Conversations Project (www.publicconversations.org), recently renamed Essential Partners, began in 1989 based on a family therapy model. The PCP rejects the binary notion of opposition and also distinguishes dialogue from debate. However, they preselect their participants and their seating arrangement places opponents next to each other. They develop the process internally with the participants, and are more regimented in their go-round or popcorn method of having participants answer specific predetermined questions. PCP can also involve brainstorming for solutions.

Civil Dialogue shares a similar goal of seeking mutual understanding. Founders Herzig and Chasin (2006) note: "In history and civics classes in the U.S., debate and political activity are presented as time-honored tools in the toolbox of democracy" (p. 1). However, in Civil Dialogue, the participants are not known in advance as the general public is invited; we make an effort, but do not recruit to ensure there are advocates on all sides of a controversy. Civil Dialogue involves a spontaneous, free-flowing dialogue following brief opening statements and later includes questions and comments from the public; each participant is not required to answer specific predetermined questions. We do concur with their goal, as lofty as it sounds:

> Dialogue has a vital if quieter, role to play in a resilient and civil democratic society. It can build bridges across divides in the body politic. It can promote healing in small communities that are struggling with controversy. It can also reduce the likelihood of gridlock in the halls of Congress, hatred in the arena of public opinion, and potentially dangerous misrepresentations in our sound-bite saturated media (p. 1).

Civil Dialogue seeks to be the first step in this process. While we have involved politicians and many have recommended the Civil Dialogue format be taken to our representatives in Washington, we believe teaching and modeling civility on a grass roots level will, over time, change the ugly tone of politics today.

Begun in 1995, the World Café (www.worldcafe.org) can include hundreds of people. A large room is divided into tables seating three or four others, a café table, if you will, within a larger conversational context. Each round is prompted by a question on a larger, overarching topic. At a predetermined moment each participant changes conversational partners by changing tables, so that no one repeats being at a table with the same participants twice. Based on seven integrated design principles, participants share ideas in an exponential way and they are graphically recorded, or "harvested," at the conclusion of the conversations. As easy and practical as this format seems, the notion of civility does not appear on their radar screen. Their format is based on predetermined questions and there is no direct accountability to a public larger than one's own table, as is the case in Civil Dialogue.

In a similar vein, the Socrates Café or Democracy Café (1996) (www.philosopher.org) discusses issues of a philosophical nature. Leaders work to keep the discourse in the realm of the philosophical nature of the question being discussed and the implications within it. Questions are determined once the group has gathered and the focus is on questioning and questioning techniques. Again, this format does not work to promote civility, but instead focuses on philosophical inquiry.

Harrison Owen developed Open Space World (www.openspaceworld.org) in 1999 focusing on the circle as the geometry of human communication. It is a self-managed format, without a planning committee, facilitator, or conference management team. Focusing on laughter and coffee breaks, OSW is outcome based with a series of plenary sessions and small group breakout sessions. Participants are urged to follow Owen's "Law of Two Feet—if a participant is neither learning nor contributing, move."

Civil Dialogue does not use the circle, as that can often single out individuals, but places panelists in a semicircle facing the audience. While laughter has characterized many a Civil Dialogue, it is not a primary tenet. Civil Dialogue is not outcome based and movement during the dialogue is minimal. No plenary sessions are held and there are no extended coffee breaks for socialization; the goal of civil dialogue is to promote civil communication.

Many formats have sprung from educational settings. The Public Dialogue Consortium (www.publicdialog.org) was established by W. Barnett Pearce when as a faculty member at the University of Massachusetts he became aware that the campus was experiencing ugly incidents of racial and political strife. The university administration crafted a civility commission to "work out ways for diverse opinions to be expressed in constructive, rather than destructive ways" (Pearce & Littlejohn, 1997, p. 197). As the format developed and the project moved to California with a basis at DeAnza College, the members of PDC envisioned "the type of persons required to thrive in the contemporary era, of the forms of communication that create spaces for transformative peacemaking, and the type of society in which they would like to live and work" (p. 198). Created by a lose connection of educators, the PDC was based on systematic questioning, appreciative inquiry, reflecting, and hypothesizing on new answers to questions (problem solving). The PCP richly relied on the communication theories of the 1980s and 1990s, but again, unlike Civil Dialogue, was created to formulate solutions to vexing problems and create an improved society.

Existing since 1988 the Intergroup Relations Education (https://igr.umich.edu), housed within their psychology and sociology programs, seeks to encourage dialogues segregated by identity group. Their mission statement, "To pursue social justice through education," works to catalyze change. To the extent that they address civility, they do so toward preventing and addressing incivility in the classroom. Obviously Civil Dialogue has a wider scope for pursuing civility. It is not limited to identity groups, its disciplinary foundation is based on communication, and Civil Dialogue does not promote social justice as a foundational tenet.

The notion of The Dialogue Process has been borrowed by many entities, from supporting public art, to financial investments, to funding mental health. One project with this title (www.dialogueproject.org) promotes Middle East dialogues in the greater New York area by focusing on the cultural differences between Israelis, Palestinians, Muslims, and non-Muslims. However, of these, the program most similar to investing in public dialogues is one based at Massachusetts Institute for Technology (www.dialogueproject.com) founded in response to the 9/11 terrorist attacks. Within an organizational setting this project focuses on lengthy formats and prepares people to use dialogue within conflict situations, with the principle that in dialogue 2 + 2 = 5. They seek to bring together people who would otherwise be unlikely to meet and work to discover how employees embrace different points of view (Isaacs, 1999). Unlike Civil Dialogue, their projects can take months instead of only a few minutes. They do not seek to model civility, but work instead to resolve conflict.

Finally, the Center for Public Deliberation (www.cpd.colostate.edu) begun by Martin Carcasson in 2006, focuses on decision making in the northern Colorado area using student facilitators to solve community problems. Based on the theory of Deliberative Inquiry (Cohen, 1989), CPD has a goal of achieving deliberative democracy. Its mission is dedicated to "enhancing local democracy through improved public communication and community problem solving" (Carcasson & Sprain, 2016, p. 44). Again, while this model is housed in communication, it relies on sorting out the nature of problems: adversarial, expert, and deliberative, and uses these in working to find community solutions. Civil Dialogue concentrates only on their notion of first-order goals (issue learning, improved democratic attitudes, improved democratic skills) (Carcasson, 2009). Again, civility is not incorporated directly into their goals. Civil Dialogue, on the other hand, has a primary eye toward civility in its process.

Obviously many practitioners have found ways to usefully employ various dialogue techniques, most attempting to solve problems embedded in their respective communities. Civil Dialogue takes a broader perspective in that no matter what type of problem, the provocative nature of Civil Dialogue can be employed wherever a multiplicity of opinions exists. It is unique from all other forums in that it works *first* to model and practice civility as a precursor to any level of agreement and/or problem solving.

This chapter has explored the theoretical underpinnings that helped inform Civil Dialogue since its inception in 2004. As we have engaged collaborators from other disciplines and worked with the format over the years, we have discovered numerous other theoretical perspectives that are relevant to Civil Dialogue and enhance its value. For example, we have relied on relevant theories at the intersection of Performance Studies and Rhetoric, where Civil Dialogue had its genesis. There are rich veins of qualitative inquiry into rhetoric, narrative, audience, ritual, small group facilitation, dialogue, and other aspects of human interaction that not only sharpen our understanding of Civil Dialogue but further validate its uniqueness and importance.

In addition, we are discovering relevant scholarship in critical pedagogy, deliberative democracy, psychology, and other disciplines and perspectives that deepen our insights into Civil Dialogue's potential in both the classroom and the commons. By continuing to examine what we mean by "civil" and "dialogue," we are constantly seeing Civil Dialogue through a new lens.

REFERENCES

Alexander, J. (2006). *The civil sphere.* Oxford, UK: Oxford.

Anderson, E. (2011). *The cosmopolitan canopy: Race and civility in everyday life.* New York, NY: W. W. Norton.

Boal, A. (1995). *The rainbow of desire: The Boal method of theatre and therapy.* London, UK: Routledge.

Bohm, D. (1996). *On dialogue.* London, UK: Routledge.

Bone, J. E., Griffin, C. L., & Scholz M. T. M. (2008). Beyond traditional conceptualizations of rhetoric: Invitational rhetoric and a move toward civility. *Western Journal of Communication, 72*: 434–462.

Brooks, D. (2010). Getting Obama right. *New York Times* (March 12): A12.

Burke, Kenneth. (1940). The rhetoric of Hitler's battle. *The Southern Review, 5*: 1–21.

Calhoun, C. (2000). The virtue of civility. *Philosophy and Public Affairs, 29*: 251–275.

Carcasson, M. (2009). *Beginning with the end in mind: A call for goal-driven deliberative practice.* New York, NY: Center for Advances in Public Engagement.

Carcasson, M., & Sprain, L. (2016). Basic problem solving: Reconceptualizing the work of public deliberation as deliberative inquiry. *Communication Theory, 26*: 41–63.

Carlson, M. (1999). *Performance: A critical introduction.* New York, NY: Routledge.

Carter, S. L. (1998). *Civility: Manners, morals, and the etiquette of democracy.* New York, NY: Basic Books.

Carter, S. L. (2011). *Is civility important?* Lecture at Yale Law School. Retrieved from vimeo.com

Chanan, Michael. (1995). *Repeated takes: A short history of recording and its effect on music.* London, UK: Verso.

Cohen, J. (1989). Deliberation and democratic legitimacy. In A. Hamlin and P. Petit (Eds.), *The good polity: Normative analysis of the state* (pp. 67–97). New York, NY: Oxford.

Crowley, S. (1992). Reflections on an argument that won't go away. *Quarterly Journal of Speech, 78*: 450–465.

Cuddihy, J. M. (1978). *No offense: Civil religion and Protestant taste.* New York, NY: Seabury.

Denzin, N. K. (2003). Performing [auto]ethnography politically. *Review of Education, Pedagogy & Cultural Studies, 25*: 257–278.

Fletcher, M. A. (2010). At national prayer breakfast, Obama warns against erosion of *civility. Washington Post* (February 4): 1.

Foss, S. K., & Griffin, C. L. (1995). Beyond persuasion: A proposal for an invitational rhetoric. *Communication Monographs, 62*: 2–18.

Freeley, A. J., & Steinberg, D. L. (2009). *Argumentation and debate* (12th ed.). Boston, MA: Wadsworth Cengage Learning.

Gutmann, A., & Thompson, D. (1990). Moral conflict and political consensus. In R. B. Douglas (Ed.), *Liberalism and the good.* New York, NY: Routledge.

Hague, B. N., & Loader, B. D. (1999). *Digital democracy: Discourse and decision making in the information age.* London, UK: Routledge.

Hall, J. A. (2013). *The importance of being civil.* Princeton, NJ: Princeton University Press.

Hammond, S. C., Anderson, R., & Cissna, K. N. (2003). The problematics of dialogue and power. *Communication Yearbook, 27*: 125–157.

Heidlebaugh, N. J. (2008). Invention and public dialogue: Lessons from rhetorical theories. *Communication Theory, 18*: 27–50.

Herzig, M., & Chasin, L. (2006). *Fostering dialogue across divides.* Watertown, MA: Public Conversations Project.

Howell, W. S. (1982). *The empathic communicator.* Belmont, CA: Wadsworth.

Isaacs, W. (1999). *Dialogue and the art of thinking together.* New York, NY: Currency.

Jackson, S. (2004). *Professing performance: Theatre in the academy from philology to performativity.* New York, NY: Cambridge University Press.

Jensen, J. V. (1981). *Argumentation: Reasoning in communication.* New York, NY: Van Nostrand.

Kim, J., & Kim, E. J. (2008). Theorizing dialogic deliberation: Everyday political talk as communicative action and dialogue. *Communication Theory, 18*: 51–70.

Kingwell, M. (1995). *A civil tongue: Justice, dialogue and the politics of pluralism.* University Park, PA: Pennsylvania State University Press.

Lozano-Reich, N. M., & Cloud, D. L. (2009). The uncivil tongue: Invitational rhetoric and the problem of inequality. *Western Journal of Communication, 73*: 220–226.

National issues forum: An overview. (2014). Dayton, OH: NIF Institute.

Neisser, P., & Hess, J. (2012). *You're not as crazy as I thought (But you're still wrong)*. Washington, DC: Potomac.

Obama, B. H. (2011). Remarks. *Arizona Republic* (January 13): A14.

Ong, W. J. (2000). *The presence of the word: Some prolegomena for cultural and religious history*. Binghamton, NY: Global.

Pearce, W. B., & Littlejohn, S. W. (1997). *Moral conflict, when social worlds collide*. Thousand Oaks, CA: Sage.

Portelli, A. (1994). *The text and the voice: Writing, speaking, and democracy in American literature*. New York, NY: Columbia University Press.

Rawls, J. (1971). *A theory of justice*. Cambridge, MA: Harvard University Press.

Stewart, J. (2011). *Bridges not walls: A book about interpersonal communication* (11th ed.). New York, NY: McGraw-Hill.

Watzlawick, P., Weakland, J., & Fisch, R. (Eds.). (1974). *Change: The principles of problem formation and problem resolution*. New York, NY: W. W. Norton.

Yankelovich, Daniel. (2004). Talking with the enemy: A series to help Americans bridge the bitter red-blue divide. *Christian Science Monitor* (October 22). Retrieved from www.cs-monitor.com/2004/1015/p10s02-coop.html

Young, I. M. (2000). *Inclusion and democracy*. Oxford, UK: Oxford University Press.

CHAPTER THREE:
The Civil Communicator

A s Bohm contends, "Democracy is rooted in disagreement." Indeed, it is our civic responsibility to disagree with ideas and policies we believe are detrimental to us and to society as a whole. We concur with legal scholar Stephen Carter (1998) when he notes, "Civility is important to democracy itself." As Calhoun (2001) notes, "[C]ivility . . . is a basic value of social life" (p. 251). As we contend, civility has little to do with politeness. It is more closely defined by an ability to speak up when one hears ideas contrary to one's own. To us, democracy is reflected in having the ability to openly discuss issues. Cohen (1989) and Dryzek (2000) agree that the opportunity to participate in effective deliberation is central to democratic legitimacy. Engaging in Civil Dialogue fosters relationships with differently minded people who are all essential to collective decision making in a democracy. It is these productive relationships, fostered through Civil Dialogue, that facilitate democratic progress. We believe civility is rooted in communicative acts and this chapter identifies the key characteristics of what we believe is necessary of a civil communicator.

HONESTY

Civility is in large part about being honest, first to oneself, and secondly, with others, especially those with whom you disagree. We each have strongly held attitudes, values, and beliefs which are at the core of many of our positions on issues as global as human change in the environment to local issues which only may affect members of our immediate community. Only when we have sorted out our feelings with our self can we present an honest portrayal of what our feelings are and how we reached them. So, initially we must be honest with ourself. On more than one occasion, participants of Civil Dialogue have expressed that the provocative statement and dialogue that followed evoked a deep thinking process that pushed them to evaluate their values and beliefs about the topic of discussion. Some have reported that they found themselves not really knowing what they thought about something but being open and willing to learn more from others. This is an honest moment of reflection as a civil communicator.

Secondly, we must honestly disclose our opinions to others. As Carter (2011) suggests, when we are civil we are not pretending, we accept each other as equals. This means welcoming the disagreement that often happens on critical issues in society. Disclosing our ideas to others does not need to mean forcing our opinions on others or even attempting to persuade them to our viewpoint; it merely means sharing candidly our viewpoints and our feelings associated with them.

Honesty is a key ingredient to civility. When we can publicly own our personal thoughts and feelings and show mutual respect for the thoughts and feelings of others with reverence and positivity, we are acting civilly.

CONSCIOUS OF LANGUAGE CHOICES

The one means we all have to communicate is through our language. While we all have different capacities for language, it is when we linguistically formulate our ideas that they become understandable by others. Many experiences go into the language choices we make: our education, our affiliations, our peers, and especially the media we attend to.

Often our ideas can become circumscribed by what we hear in the media. We hear a certain phrase, such as one used by a politician or in an advertisement, and once it is repeated often enough, it becomes part of our own speech, many times without us ever being aware of it. Civility is consciously choosing words that are your own. This means being aware of terms that may belittle or even demonize others, or words than can oversimplify a multifaceted problem. Carcasson and Sprain (2016 p. 46) warn against simplification in our language by using magic bullets (assuming there is one solution to a complex problem), choosing devil figures/scapegoats (assuming the problem is caused by one individual or entity), or paradox splitting (focusing only on one side of an issue while ignoring the other). Words can be paradoxical in meaning, creating as much confusion as they do clarity.

Words themselves have great power. To practice civility, it is necessary to choose one's words carefully and thoughtfully. A basic understanding of language is a key component to not offending others with one's language choices, while still genuinely making one's point. It is our civic duty to be cognizant of the word choices we make and especially how they may impact others. It is once we are aware of the power of language that our speech becomes truly civil.

BEING MULTIPRESENT

Whereas many psychologists, athletic coaches, and even life coaches may encourage one to "be in the moment," as your civility coaches we cannot recommend such a narrow view. Our thought patterns stem from our past history, consume our present, and cloud our future. Being civil means bringing a wider perspective to a situation of disagreement.

Initially, the civil communicator must be cognizant of the past, both one's own and the historical past. Toward this end, this person must be educated on the nuances of a conflict and how his or her position came to be formed in that conflict. Much like a basketball coach who encourages a slumping athlete not to consider the last four missed shots when the player is open and the game is on the line, even though that is a significant part of one's history, one cannot help but be reminded of that when in the heat of the game. Likewise, a historical perspective of recent events and actions on an issue is also crucial to keep in mind. Without accurate knowledge, speakers can often just shoot from the hip, saying anything that comes to mind, without regard for the veracity of the truth. While not all members of society share the same amount of common knowledge regarding a controversy, and that knowledge may vary depending upon one's value system, possessing a general understanding of an issue is typically a precursor to an invitation to dialogue. A civil communicator is aware of his or her own past, as well as the historical past, and knows how it shapes the ideas likely to come out of one's mouth.

Likewise, a civil communicator needs to be comfortable and confident in expressing viewpoints and hearing alternatives in the present. Often, psychologists and life coaches will prescribe breathing exercises or meditation to be able to "stay in the present." Yet our minds continue to work in overdrive, especially in times when we experience conflict—a natural defense mechanism kicks in when we feel threatened. This means that focusing exclusively on the present endangers our dialogues by having too narrow a focus. Instead, we need to be aware that every member of the dialogue brings to it a rich tapestry of experiences, not unlike our own, which will shape the direction, tenor, and meaning of the dialogue, and our focus should remain with the speaker, as tempting as it is to mentally plan out how we intend to respond.

Toward this end, a civil communicator is constantly contemplative about the future, reflecting on how one's word choices, stories, and positions may affect others who do not share these experiences and may have varying opinions. One must always keep an awareness of one's potential impact on others, being comfortable and confident that one's purpose may or may not be persuasive in nature. As such, having one eye on the future will likely shape our current behavior through our language choices, reactions to other individuals, and our reactions to a host of differing viewpoints. One must be careful to select words that will not likely offend or cause others to react defensively, while maintaining the integrity of truthfully expressing our own viewpoints. Being civil requires one to be in all three places: past, present, and future, simultaneously; it is a difficult, but not impossible task.

CONSCIOUS OF CHANGE

By its very nature, Aristotle argues that all rhetoric is persuasive. Hence any position that we make has the ability to persuade others or even to strengthen our own viewpoint through self-persuasion. For one to engage in a Civil Dialogue, one needs to be aware of this fact and hence be willing to be an open participant in the process of persuasion. As such, a civil communicator is capable of changing others and, in turn, being changed. Civil communicators have the facility to impact others with their knowledge and experiences. Even unintentionally, dialogue can influence others' viewpoints.

While acknowledging the potential of influencing others, the civil communicator must simultaneously be aware of being under the spell of influence from others. Contrary opinions can lead to clash, yet civil communicators are confident that just as they are potential agents of change, so are they changeable. In Maslow's words, we are "always in the process of becoming." Hence as fixed as some of our attitudes, values, and beliefs may be, listening to, recognizing, and acknowledging differing points of view has the capacity to change who we are. To engage in Civil Dialogue opens us to this possibility. As such, most all of our viewpoints are constantly in a state of flux. And while Civil Dialogue does not require a consensus, or any degree of change, change is often the result. We admit that compromise is not at issue; no one needs to politely demur to another's position for the sake of nicety. In fact, as Gutmann and Thompson (2004) argue, deliberation does not make differences suddenly compatible, but it can help participants recognize the moral merit in an opponent's claim, thereby fostering mutual respect and reciprocity. It is this respect that is an essential ingredient in civility. Since decision making per se is not at the core of Civil Dialogue, change in any degree is a possibility, but not a foregone conclusion.

Many might argue that to effect significant change, some degree of incivility must occur. Often titled "civil disobedience," political scientist Joel Olson (2007) writes that "zealots have often presented their actions as advancing democracy rather than threatening it" (p. 686). He uses as his example American abolitionists who regularly broke up church services, defied laws of racial segregation, and called for the breakup of the Union some 20 years before the Civil War. By identifying their actions as religious fundamentalism Olson writes, "Zealotry is not undemocratic in temperament. Rather it is a strategy used to win political struggles, whose aim and outcome may or may not be democratic" (p. 686). He identifies fanatics as irrational, intolerant, as akin to fundamentalism and terrorism. Zealotry contends there is no middle ground. In describing abolitionists, Olson remarked, "Garrisonian zealotry did not oppose rational deliberation or empirical evidence and indeed made good use of both" (p. 686). Relying on Voltaire's conceptualization of fanaticism in the *Philosophical Dictionary*, Olson concludes that it "turns an unhealthy urge into an obsession . . . which represents disharmony, immoderation, irrationality and intolerance" (p. 687).

In his discussion Olson (2007) further comments that fanatics are incapable of empathy, obsessed with purity, and driven by hatred, indeed even wanting destruction. It is here where the lines of political and ideological divide separate. Here is where Olson points to multiple references of the 9/11 terrorist activities, which sought to destroy the United States. In civil disobedience, there is no middle ground, no reasoning with advocates who hold alternate viewpoints. Indeed, even the *Oxford English Dictionary* defines moderation as "convergence to the position of the median voter." Civil disobedience presents only a bipolar framework, in Olson's case study, Abolitionists vs. Unionists. He points to the friends/enemies dichotomy as an attempt to push people off the fence (p. 693).

One could easily identify several examples of civil disobedience which may seem warranted: vegan fanatics, PETA, the bra-burning women of the 1970s. However, the recent controversy concerning marriage equality defies the contemporary success of civil disobedience. In the post-Stonewall era, gays and lesbians attempted civil disobedience in numerous ways. The first gay pride parades were known for extremists, cross-dressing nuns, dykes on bikes, etc. For most people, their first exposure to gay life was by viewing such parades on television, or hearing of civil disobedience of ACT UP, a gay rights organization striving to gain attention for the AIDS crisis of the 1980s. Indeed, it was these stereotypes of extremism, combined with the gut-wrenching scenes of gay men withering away from AIDS, that first characterized what gay life was all about. Once a court decision legitimizing marriage rights was handed down in Hawaii in 1996, society revolted. Not only was it quickly put to voters before the decision even took effect, it triggered the national Defense of Marriage Act (DOMA) which was overwhelming approved by both House and Senate and signed immediately by President Clinton, specifying that marriage was between one man and one woman.

When the first same-sex weddings ultimately occurred in 2004 as a result of a court decision in Massachusetts, proponents sought to project images of solemnity, portraying the discrimination of having been denied marriage rights for so long. Solomon (2014) writes that consistent with their preconception of gay and lesbians, the media cameras were looking for scenes that viewers would find outrageous or provocative. However, in working to ensure that the state legislature would not overturn the ruling, Solomon notes that "one thing that could break through the fear was allowing lawmakers to get to know married [gay] couples and their families. When they did, they would understand viscerally that these families were not much different from their own and that they should treat gay families as they'd want their own families treated"

(p. 97). This was especially true of legislators who represented rural districts. Indeed, one early convert encouraged, "[O]ne of the best things I can tell you to do is to become more visible in your community" (p. 105). Another legislator admitted, "[I]t was meeting the children of a few gay couples that did it" (p. 106). Evan Wolfson, founder of Freedom to Marry, and the architect of the national marriage equality movement (as espoused in his 1983 masters thesis) noted that a more civil approach to marriage equality was essential as he often concluded his speeches, "Let us build a new approach, partnership, tools, and entities that can reach the middle and bring it all home" (p. 111). Without a doubt Wolfson understood that what was necessary to achieve success was a critical mass of public support. By taking an issue the American public overwhelming agreed upon through the early 2000s (opposition to marriage equality) and changing that perception, one conversation at a time, with legislators, civic leaders, national politicians, and family members, the Freedom to Marry message was finally institutionalized by the Supreme Court in 2015 in *Obergefell v. Hodges*; it was far ahead of the organization's earlier stated goal to win marriage equality in 10 states by 2020. Clearly it was demonstrating the humanity of the issue, which was key to keeping marriage equality in play through a volatile legislative and referenda process. Solomon ultimately concluded that marriage equality was won by gays and lesbians showing "raw emotion, some tears. . .and a rededication to sharing their own stories" (p. 118).

What this example demonstrates is that there are many ways to instigate change, even when discussing vexing problems; and that being a civil communicator is at the core of such effective change. However, whether or not change happens, a civil communicator is clearly aware that change is a possibility, change in a variety of directions. A civil communicator is cognizant that as the result of participating in dialogue, he or she may change viewpoints based on the narratives and opinions of others and/or that his or her comments may well effect change in another. Oftentimes this change is not immediate, but is part of an incremental process that leads people to support various viewpoints. Indeed, even the most ardent supporter of a cause may well temper opinions to be more centrist after carefully listening to oppositional advocates state their claims. Whether or not change happens is not crucially relevant to civil communication. It is the process and the potential for change that all participants are aware could occur from the process that characterizes a Civil Dialogue.

CONSCIOUS OF STYLE

We are all aware of people who when they express themselves sound more authoritative, or arrogant, or even timid than other people. Each of us has our own unique communicator style. Norton (1978) defines communicator style as: "The way one verbally and paraverbally interacts to signal how literal meaning should be taken, interpreted, filtered, or understood" (p. 99). He has divided communicator styles into nine subconstructs: dominance, dramatic, contentious, animated, impression leaving, relaxed, attentive, open, and friendly. We typically evaluate people based on these factors to rate their communicator style. But have you ever stopped to think of what you sound like when you dialogue with others? Just as we judge others, we are constantly being judged as well, and civil communicators are aware of how they present their ideas within a Civil Dialogue.

Think back to the few times when you became aware of your communicator style. Perhaps it was being video recorded for a public speaking class, or it may have been the first time you heard your own voice played back to you. Chances are, you were not favorably impressed and wondered, is that really what I sound and look like? No doubt, our communicator style derives from a number of factors. Many characteristics may be biologically determined as Horvath (1995) found in his study of twins. Some are also likely the result of the environment in which we were raised, perhaps an accent or certain cadence punctuates our speech. Our word choices may result from our exposure to others as well as the media. Regardless of how we acquired our communicator style, it is wise to be aware of how others perceive our style when we seek to speak civilly.

Researchers have linked communicator style to a variety of factors: sex differences (Montgomery & Norton, 1981); management style (Sager, 2008); teacher effectiveness (Kirk, 2011); and more recently, even bullying behavior (Dursun & Akbulut, 2012). While these links are significant, perhaps we can learn the most about our own style by returning to Norton's (1983) constructs and doing a quick self-inventory. How dominant are we in conversations? Do we always need the first and last word? Do we express our ideas dramatically, or are we more casual in tone? Do others perceive us and our ideas as contentious, highly controversial, or outside the mainstream; or are we fairly impartial in the way we present our thoughts and experiences? How animated are we? Do we have exaggerated facial expressions or expansive gestures when speaking, or are we more reticent and understated? Do others remember our ideas long after a dialogue has occurred, or is what we say easily forgotten? Do we appear relaxed as a speaker, confident in presenting our ideas, or do we exhibit signs of nervousness, fidgeting, etc.? Do we present an open posture, welcoming others, or are we more closed off (i.e., crossing our legs and arms to shut out others' ideas)? Finally, do we come across as friendly, or cold? While there is an extreme on each side of the poles of these behaviors, each of us is likely to fall somewhere away from the poles and more to the center. Yet, these constructs are important to consider as we participate in Civil Dialogues, as the way we construct and present a message may well be interpreted as importantly as the message itself. Being conscious of our own style, especially if we tend to typify extreme behaviors, is crucial to welcoming others into dialogue and is a key to civil communication.

OWNING RESPONSIBILITY

Engaging in civil communication means respecting yourself and your ideas enough to test them in the free marketplace of ideas. It is critical to be comfortable with the positions we espouse. Engaging in Civil Dialogue can even help us to give voice to our opinions, especially if we are undecided or neutral about a certain issue. Actually hearing words come out of our mouth based on what we may know or feel is a crucial benefit to the Civil Dialogue process.

However, we should not just use others as a testing ground to gauge our opinions; we must be prepared to take ownership of the ideas we present. Iris Young (2000), in her discussion of inclusive political communication writes, "Participants in the processes of communication must be reasonable in the sense of willing to be accountable to others" (p. 52). As humans, we are a composite of not only all the physical features that comprise us, but also of all the ideas, thoughts, and words that we use to express those thoughts and feelings. As such, it is incumbent upon us to take ownership of our own ideas, and not merely present the ideas of others as our own. To do so risks being inauthentic to ourselves and to the dialogue process. After participating in a chair during a dialogue we hosted, a woman remarked, "I realize that I have no opinions of my own, all I hear is my mother's voice coming out of my mouth." For her, that was a startling realization. For years, she had parroted her mother's viewpoints without thinking for herself and without having to take ownership of her own ideas. It is only when we are faced with being confronted on our ideas that we can willingly learn to take ownership of them. Such confrontation may also take the form of being asked difficult questions from the audience or another panelist. Instead of shying away from such questions, a civil communicator seeks to provide clarity about his or her ideas, and does not seek to shift position away from having to answer such difficult questions. Being willing to answer difficult questions is key to civil behavior for it provides a paradigm for others to follow.

WILLINGNESS TO LIVE WITH DISAGREEMENT

The very nature of living in a democracy presumes that we will be governed by the will of the majority. As such, we will not always get our way, the candidates we support will not always win, lawmakers will enact legislation with which we disagree, and courts will hand down decisions we deem to be unfair. Perhaps being a civil communicator is the first step in learning to live in a democracy, for if we can acknowledge that our society will not completely model the world in which we hope to live, and yet we choose to live in that society anyway, we can best live civilly.

As political scientists have pointed out, exposure to political disagreement makes people better understand opposing political viewpoints, which leads to greater political tolerance (Mutz, 2002) and increases political knowledge if people approach the process with open minds (Barabas, 2004). Indeed, open minds require open hearts to accept the will of the majority. Knowing that we and "our side" will not always "win" in the court of public opinion and policy, we must graciously accept that notion so that we can engage in civil communication. For if we forestall civil behaviors, in essence refuse to do our jobs as citizens and elected officials, there is likely to be little progress made toward sharing our reasoning and our desire for understanding and potential change. Knowing that we will have dialogues with people who vehemently disagree with us, sometimes fundamentally with values we hold sacred, and still being willing to put our opinions into the public forum, knowing that change is not immediately likely, is a necessary characteristic of a civil communicator.

Purposely, there's been little written in this chapter about how to manage or resolve conflict, merely how to comport oneself in a civil manner. We acknowledge that a fundamental necessity for Civil Dialogue is for there to be some inherent conflict at issue. Carcasson and Sprain (2016) prefer to put the locus of the nature of conflict on the problem, by defining what they term "wicked problems." In their theory of public deliberation, they conclude: "Simply explaining the nature of wicked problems before a deliberative event can have an inoculation effect, as citizens realize that wickedness is inherent to the problem and its competing values rather than assigning wickedness to opposing groups" (p. 50). Though we recognize that in society people are often deemed wicked and may even demonize themselves for holding certain beliefs, we concur and prefer to place the blame squarely on the vexing nature of the complex problem. As such, people who hold opinions about such a topic are not inherently themselves wicked. We contend that productive dialogue about conflict is central to modeling civil communication skills. It is when one has mastered the skills of both speaking and listening within this framework that true democracy can take place. Civil communication requires nothing less.

REFERENCES

Aristotle. (2007). *On rhetoric: A theory of civic discourse* (2nd ed.). Trans. George A. Kennedy. New York, NY: Oxford University.

Barabas, J. (2004). How deliberation affects policy opinions. *American Political Science Review,* 98: 687–701.

Bohm, D. (1996). *On dialogue.* London, UK: Routledge.

Calhoun, C. (2000). The virtue of civility. *Philosophy and Public Affairs,* 29: 251–275.

Carcasson, M., & Sprain, L. (2106). Beyond problem solving: Reconceptualizing the work of public deliberation as deliberative inquiry. *Communication Theory,* 26: 41–63.

Carter, S. L. (1998). *Civility: Manners, morals, and the etiquette of democracy.* New York, NY: Basic Books.

Carter, S. L. (2011). *Is civility important?* Lecture at Yale Law School. Retrieved from vimeo.com

Cohen, J. (1989). Deliberation and democratic legitimacy. In A. Hamlin & P. Petit (Eds.), *The good polity: Normative analysis of the state* (pp. 67–91). New York, NY: Oxford University Press.

Downs, C. W., Archer, J., McGrath, J., & Stafford, J. (1988). An analysis of communication style instrumentation: Norton's communicator style measure Richmond and McCroskey's management communication style scale Duran & Wheeless's communicative adaptability scale; Self-reference measures Mok's communication styles survey example Klauss and Bass's focal person's communication survey/colleague questionnaire focal persons communication style. *Management Communication Quarterly, 1*: 543–572.

Dryzek, J. S. (2000). Deliberative democracy and beyond: Liberals, critics, contestations. New York, NY: Oxford University Press.

Dursun, O. O., & Akbulut, Y. (2012). Communicator style as a predictor of cyberbullying in hybrid learning environments. *Turkish Online Journal of Qualitative Inquiry, 3*.

Gutmann, A., & Thompson, D. (2004). *Why deliberative democracy?* Princeton, NJ: Princeton University Press.

Horvath, C. W. (1995). Biological origins of communicator style. *Communication Quarterly, 43*: 394–407.

Kirk, D. D. (2011). Style and satisfaction: An examination of the relationship between instructor communicator style and instructor job satisfaction. Unpublished Ph.D. dissertation. Denton, TX: University of North Texas.

Maslow, A. H. (1943). A theory of human motivation. *Psychological Review, 50*: 370–396.

Montgomery, B. M., & Norton, R. W. (1981). Sex differences and similarities in communicator style. *Communication Monographs, 48*: 121–132.

Mutz, D. (2002). Cross-cutting social networks: Testing democratic theory in practice. *American Political Science Review, 96*: 111–126.

Norton, R. (1978). Foundation of a communicator style construct. *Human Communication Research, 4*: 99–111.

Norton, R. (1983). *Communicator style; theory application, and measures.* Beverly Hills, CA: Sage.

Olson, J. (2007). The freshness of fanaticism: The abolitionist defense of zealotry. *Perspectives on Politics, 5*: 685–701.

Pfau, M. (1997). The inoculation model of resistance to influence. In F. J. Boster & G. Barnett (Eds.), *Progress in communication sciences* (vol. 13, pp. 133–171). Norwood, NJ: Ablex.

Sager, K. L. (2008). An exploratory study of the relationship between theory X/Y assumptions and superior communicator style. *Management Communication Quarterly, 22*: 288–312.

Solomon, M. (2014). *Winning marriage, the inside story of how same-sex couples took on the politicians and pundits—and won.* Lebanon, NH: University Press of New England.

Voltaire. (1962). *Philosophical dictionary.* Trans. Peter Gay. New York, NY: Basic.

CHAPTER FOUR:
Civil Listening

Perhaps no skill is more important in a public setting than the ability to civilly listen to others. We have come to appreciate the degree to which Civil Dialogue is not just about speaking our minds, but also about listening. In fact, scholars have observed that civility includes specific properties such as "civil listening" skills: "Many of the beneficial by-products for democracy that we associate with conflict cannot occur unless people who disagree are willing to listen to one another, which can only be accomplished when disagreement is combined with civility" (Mutz, 2006). Rhetors who practice civil listening skills go beyond what is typically characterized as "empathic listening" (Howell, 1982) or "dialogic listening" (Stewart, Zediker, & Witteborn, 2011) and seek to discover "how" another is experiencing life through particular skills of restatement and questioning. Civil listeners also do not listen only with an ear toward crafting their own debatable response, critical to one's burden of rebuttal (Jensen, 1981). Rather, civil listening involves respecting another's viewpoint, even when one does not agree, acknowledging the notion of difference without opposition, and seeks to understand not merely "how" the other is feeling but moving to specific motivations as to "why" another is experiencing a divergent viewpoint. As such, civility involves a balance of both speaking and listening. In short, civility is as much about listening to divergent viewpoints as it is about clearly communicating one's own thoughts and beliefs.

There are several skills that make civil listening unique from the types of listening we do in our everyday relationships. While it is typically always more fun to share our opinion, the act of civil communication requires key listening skills that often must be learned and practiced.

BARRIERS TO CIVIL LISTENING

Unfortunately, while most of us have received training in a variety of communication skills, little attention is often paid to improving listening behaviors. This may seem odd given that we spend proportionately more time listening than we do reading, speaking, or writing (Nichols & Stevens, 1957), yet our formal education has focused extensively on teaching us these latter skills. Additionally, humans possess a unique skill of being able to listen and process words much faster than they can be spoken. While most people speak at approximately 125 to 150 words per minute, our brain can understand and process up to 1,000 words per minute. This leaves plenty of mental time and space for us to attend to other topics or issues, to daydream; or we can choose to use that extra brain power to focus on our civil listening skills. What typically results for most people is that instead of remembering large amounts of what a speaker says, early research has shown (Nichols & Stevens, 1957) and has been confirmed (Bolton, 1979; Stauffer, Frost, & Rybolt, 1983) that we are only able to retain about 25% of what we hear, no matter how hard we try. Why do we have such a difficult time focusing on and improving our listening skills?

There are three misconceptions about listening. Initially, many of us believe that listening is a natural process. If that were true, we would either be born good listeners or not; there would be little we could do to improve our listening behaviors. This is simply not true. Secondly, it is often believed that listening and hearing are the same thing. Humans typically have little control over what they hear; sounds within a certain decibel range are audible. On the other hand, listening is largely a process of discriminating and identifying which sounds are meaningful and important to us and which aren't. We have to learn how to listen. Listening is a consciously purposive activity for which we need systematic training to do well. Finally, even when we listen to a speaker, every person responds a bit differently to what is said based on their opinions and past experiences. We don't all respond identically, even to identical words. Unfortunately, the act of listening is not a visible one; we can't physically see anyone listening. Certainly people can give us nonverbal cues that they are listening—an attentive face, nodding of the head, for example—but even these clues can be misleading, especially when engaged in listening to information we may have a hard time accepting into our own frame of reference.

When listening to an idea which we may find unfamiliar or difficult to accept, it is natural to engage in one of the types of nonlistening behaviors.

TYPES OF NONLISTENING BEHAVIORS

Communication scholars Brooks and Emmert (1976) have identified seven typical patterns nonlisteners fall into, as follows:

Pseudolistening. These are people who give the appearance of being attentive, with smiles, head-nods, minimal responses, etc., outwardly giving all the nonverbal cues that they are listening, but behind this polite facade, they are ignoring or not attending to the other person.

Stagehogging. These are people who are only interested in expressing their own ideas, and don't care about what others have to say on the subject. They have not embraced the purpose of civil listening, instead are intent only on giving short speeches about their opinions.

Selective listening. Selective listeners only listen to the parts of a message that interest them and may support their point of view rejecting or ignoring everything else. Selective listeners have their own agenda of interesting and valuable topics and disregard or are disinterested in others' agendas.

Insulated listening. The opposite of selective listeners, insulated listeners are people who actively avoid or ignore certain topics, particularly when issues become heated or controversial. When a hot topic arises in conversation, they turn off their listening skills, refusing to believe that there are alternative points of view from their own.

Defensive listening. People who take innocent comments as personal attacks on themselves or their position are defensive listeners. Defensive listening creates impressions of insecurity and a lack of confidence.

Ambushing. Ambushers are people who listen very carefully. However, they do so to collect information that can be used against another person (like a cross-examining attorney). These people are constantly looking to ambush and trap the others in their own ideas and words, usually to prove or support a strong personal belief of their own. Ambushing is a form of debate and causes others to be defensive.

Insensitive listening. While rare, there are people who are not able to listen beyond the face value of the other's words. These people have difficulty picking up on hidden meanings, sarcasm, or subtle nonverbal cues.

WHAT CIVIL LISTENING IS NOT

Most types of listening presume that those involved in the listening process are engaged in a longer term interpersonal relationship. Counselors have identified therapeutic settings for listening for romantic couples or family members to improve their relational skills. Social philosophers have opined about different perspectives listeners can take and behaviors related to those perspectives to aid listening in classrooms, among friends, coworkers, and within a larger business setting. What we find unique about civil listening situations is that many times, the people engaged in listening are from the public and are likely strangers, or at least little-known acquaintances, with whom you are unlikely to form long-term interpersonal relationships. As such, respecting and listening to different viewpoints is very different from what other scholars have written about listening behaviors.

CIVIL LISTENING IS DISTINCT FROM EMPATHIC LISTENING

One of the most common types of listening behavior is "empathic listening." In one of the first books on empathy, *The Empathic Communicator,* William Howell (1982) defined empathy as "[t]he ability to replicate what you perceive another to be feeling or thinking" (p. 245). Moreover, psychologist Kenneth Clark (1980) articulated that empathy is "the capacity of an individual to feel the needs, the aspirations, the frustrations, the joy, the sorrows, the anxieties, the hurt, indeed, the hunger of others as if they were his own" (p. 188). Noted humanistic psychologist Carl Rogers (1980) expanded this concept to include empathic listening as: "To be with another . . . that for the time being, you lay aside your own views and values in order to enter another's world without prejudice. In some sense it means that you lay aside yourself" (pp. 142–143). In essence, empathy means that you use your listening skills to actually feel what the other person feels, as though you are experiencing it yourself.

While we acknowledge that there are certain times when empathic listening is an essential skill, we argue that many times it is not possible. In instances when you are being confronted with information and experiences that are new, or with which you may disagree, *feeling* a like experience is nearly impossible. Without understanding why someone holds a certain position, it is difficult to imagine what it feels like to be them. Many times, in civil communication, others may hold opinions that are so different from our own that it is impossible to be empathic, for that would require one to take a position that is wholly different from their own. Each of us is the product of all our past experiences, training, upbringing, and education and have planned many of our future courses of action. It is typically impossible to "lay aside yourself" given one's own attitudes, expectations, education, past experiences, and values that shape their worldview. When asked to share those in a public forum it would be unreasonable to expect that everyone might "feel," or even be capable of feeling the same way you do.

Furthermore, empathic listening typically requires one to engage in mirroring or restating another person's feelings or opinions, trying to be as accurate as possible in reflecting what the other just said. This process continues with a series of questions about perception checking: "Is that what you meant?" "Am I understanding you correctly?" and continuing the process until you receive an affirmative answer (Stewart, Zediker, & Witteborn, 2009). In civil listening situations, often the flow of interaction is much quicker than in a two-person conversation, with multiple people wishing to weigh in on an issue. In these fast-paced interactions, paraphrasing would only serve to slow the process and not allow for multiple participants to share their reactions to a speaker as well as present their own ideas. Obviously in the context of a public dialogue, not only would a paraphrasing exchange be time consuming, it would typically leave out other panelists and the audience, unless they were on the same wavelength as the listener. In a timed round of Civil Dialogue, or even in situations where respectful civil listening occurs, time does not permit, nor would it be appropriate to attempt to engage in what would likely be an artificial form of listening behavior.

CIVIL LISTENING IS DISTINCT FROM DIALOGIC LISTENING

Another viewpoint on listening behavior is referred to as "dialogic listening" (Bakhtin, 1986). Also known as "responsive listening" (Shotter, 2009) and "mindful listening" (Shafir, 2000), these forms of listening focus on creating a dialogic moment which requires a connection or joint action between speaker and listener in which the "listener becomes the speaker" (Bakhtin, 1986). Dialogic listening implies that listeners deductively anticipate the intent of a speaker's meaning. Shotter (2009) suggests that in this process of cocreation we respond to another "in an anticipatory fashion" (p. 26). Merleau-Ponty (1962) goes so far as to note "my world is carried forward by lines of intentionality which trace out in advance at least the style of what is to come" (pp. 416–417). Civil listening presupposes no such requirement. Being in dialogue with another, typically unfamiliar, person, listening to his or her ideas for the first time it is impossible to *anticipate*, even stylistically, what the person may say or how the person may say it. Likewise, a speaker cannot anticipate how one's thoughts and opinions will be interpreted by all respective listeners, as each person witnessing a dialogue will likely respond differently. The goals of dialogic listening are valuable to comprehend in order to achieve equitable and invitational orientation toward others, but in a practical Civil Dialogue listening moment, they are not likely to occur. Instead, as speakers to an audience, we selectively choose what feedback to attend to, typically feedback that is sympathetic or similar to our own viewpoint. The reversal of speaker and listener is a contradiction in practice given the context of the provocation and disagreement that Civil Dialogue produces.

While the Civil Dialogue process encourages everyone to build on one another's comments, neither the facilitator, the panelists, nor the audience are able to anticipate what is likely to occur by listening to participants. In that respect, each dialogue is unique, and no one is able to forecast the collective product of speakers and listeners interacting at that moment in time.

Furthermore, dialogic listening necessitates a "change in one's way of seeing things" (Katz & Shotter, 1998) predicated on overcoming what Wittgenstein (1980) calls difficulties of the will.

Explicit here is the notion of change occurring, which is counter to the original intention of Civil Dialogue. During the process of civil listening change *may* occur, but it is not a prerequisite; the goals are mutual understanding and practicing civil behavior. Indeed, one may be so thoroughly convicted in their strongly agree/disagree position that no change is a distinct possibility. It is highly possible that good listeners can and will keep their own ground, even after hearing heartfelt information to the contrary. We found this to be particularly true when holding Civil Dialogues in conjunction with presidential debates When surveyed regarding likely voting behavior prior to a debate and after a debate, no matter which candidate was perceived as having "won" the debate, little to no change occurred in who listeners were planning to vote for (Olson, Genette, & Linde, 2013). Even if their candidate "lost," little real change occurred.

Dialogic listening was initially popularized in the organizational setting where the focus was on the importance of dialogue and listening in "learning organizations" (Stewart et al., 2009). This application presumes a certain motivation for productivity: to remain competitive in major industry (i.e., automotive, airline industries). In civil listening, there is no presumption of productivity; there is no competition to be "better than" the last dialogue, as industries need to be competitive to remain viable. Instead, the goal of productivity is replaced with the need for mutual understanding, and toward that aim civility as practiced in the given moment of the dialogue is all that is sought.

PRACTICING SKILLS OF A CIVIL LISTENER

There are several skills that make civil listening unique from the type of listening we do in our everyday relationships. While these preceding good-faith efforts may well be helpful in some situations, when engaging in civil listening, we find there to be several unique skills distinct from these other forms of listening.

To practice civil listening all parties involved must be:

1. Willing to engage. While we have little control over the rate at which someone speaks, it is essential to not be in a hurry either as speakers or listeners. In a Civil Dialogue context, willingness to engage may involve volunteering to take a chair and being a participant in the dialogue or providing a comment or example as a member of the audience. Furthermore, it is the presumption to care about the provocative issue in play during the dialogue. A civil listener is not one who appears disinterested.

2. Willing to trust and be respectful of the listening process. Civil listening is not having a speech prepared or a position ready to give. To do so only keeps one circumscribed in

one's own ideas, unwilling to appreciate the viewpoints of others. In order to engage in civil listening one must be comfortable enough with the listening process being unscripted and to go with the flow of the dialogue. Anticipating what another might say only serves to promote one's own "script" and doesn't allow participants to civilly listen to another. One doesn't just listen to the words that are spoken, but works to pay attention to the whole person, both verbally and nonverbally, carefully attuning to the nuances of "how" something is said. Civil listening involves putting aside our normal human tendency to "multitask" and instead requires us to focus completely on our listening behavior. This may prove difficult as the outcome of true civil listening is unknown from the start. Since most human interaction is based on some sort of plan or intention, civil listening is unique, in that it is agenda-less. While disagreement, conflicts, and persuasion may occur, all ulterior motives are set aside to respect whatever occurs during the process of civil listening. In essence, it's about trusting oneself to enjoy the unpredictability of the dialogue.

3. Needing and willing to have the courage to understand and be understood. There is a simultaneous action that occurs in civil listening, others comprehending one person's ideas while at the same time that person feels like his or her ideas are being received and given merit. As with trusting the process, one must also trust formulating one's own positions, not merely parroting what one may have "heard" parents, friends, politicians, or news reporters say. During civil listening, one may feel pulled in multiple directions, working to understand all the participants, even though they may have valid points of disagreement. The challenge is to synthesize the information one hears to inform and express one's *own* viewpoint. Many times, that may not occur within the brief timespan of a Civil Dialogue, but is the result of reflecting back on salient points in the dialogue, seeking additional information and working to formulate a viewpoint. It is key to note that perspectives may not be firmly held or are not static in time. With additional experience one may find his or her position constantly in a state of flux. That doesn't mean one doesn't hold a viewpoint, as one is likely to be able to articulate an opinion at any single time. Voicing one's standpoint takes courage, as we risk being challenged by others, but simultaneously being supported. Both are key tenets of civil listening.

4. Willing to withhold judgment. It is a normal human tendency to make judgments. We typically find ourselves in interpersonal situations where listening requires us to help others find solutions to their problems and come to some sense of resolution about issues that bother them. In conversations, too often multiple people will start speaking at once, with usually the loudest voice being attended to. Civil listening strives to set this human tendency aside, instead fully hearing others without making judgments or giving advice. In practice, this initially means not interrupting. One can demonstrate this with the creative use of silence. While most people in our American culture are uncomfortable with silence,

we need to resist the urge to fill conversational voids with words. The use of silence is tricky. On one hand, being silent can give another a chance to be understood; to talk at one's own pace. At the same time, silence is often assumed to mean agreement (Shotter, 2009), so it is easy to interpret someone's silence as agreement when nothing may be farther from the truth. So, how do we embrace silence? It is key to realize that while we are silent we are withholding verbal judgment. Silence prevents us from planning or speaking our own position, and allows us to fully observe the other and to consciously reflect on what was said. Given the express goal of civil communication is mutual understanding, the willingness to withhold judgments is essential to achieving this goal.

5. Willing to create a mutual venture. Civil listening involves a blending of combined resources (Howell, 1982). It is a simultaneous process that is highly dynamic, without a formal leader or follower. Instead, each person is responsible to each other. There is a tacit sense of equality among each panelist. In a formal Civil Dialogue, each speaker is given roughly the same amount of time for opening and closing remarks. After that, the facilitator works to ensure that all participants are actively able to engage so that all viewpoints are expressed. Baxter and Montgomery (1996) articulate that the primary feature of dialogue "implicate[s] a kind of in-the-moment interactive multivocality, in which multiple points of view retain their integrity as they play off each other" (p. 160). Creating this mutual venture encourages each person to share. In addition to traditional listening skills, this can be as simple as asking a speaker, "Tell me more," or just a well-placed "Oh." A speaker can easily be coaxed into continuing his or her train of thought by simple interrogatives like "Then?" or "So?" Even these minimal verbal responses indicate and ensure one's responsiveness to the speaker and demonstrate willingness to make the civil listening process a mutual one. More directly, one can even use open-ended questions, as opposed to closed-ended questions, which typically request a simple, predetermined response and often end a speaker's turn. Investing in a mutual venture with fellow panelists, audience members, and facilitator is critical in practicing civil listening.

Following all these steps is not easy, but we offer several suggestions as to how to practice being a civil listener. Initially, it is crucial to create an atmosphere of warmth and trust. Being friendly while knowing you may be encountering people who do not share your viewpoints can be tricky, as the ire of human suspicion weighs heavily. However, understanding that we have something positive to gain from each person we meet will better enable you to put these fears aside and enjoy the civil listening process.

Once the formal listening process begins, it is essential to demonstrate physical attention to your listening behavior. Demonstrating a relaxed attentiveness, leaning forward, appearing alert with positive, inquisitive, and engaged facial expressions are all signals that you're commit-

HOT TOPICS, COOL HEADS: A Handbook for Civil Dialogue

ted to the listening process. Having an "open" posture indicates you're willing to be accepting and nonjudgmental to what is said.

In Civil Dialogue, the context is created to maximize positive interaction. The five chairs are meaningfully spaced and placed to ensure that everyone is in a conversational distance and can make eye contact with each other. This is the reason we suggest using chairs stationary on the floor and cannot be wheeled apart, so people cannot physically pull away from the dialogue should issues become passionate or tense.

Reacting to the others is also key to demonstrating that one is responsive to what is being said. Engaging in distracting gestures only attracts attention away from the speaker. As someone is speaking, the focus should be on him or her visually, giving the speaker full attention and demonstrating both one's physical and psychological presence.

While it is much more difficult to provide hints to clear your mind to successfully engage in civil listening, recalling the above five steps of what one must be willing to do provides a thorough and healthy reminder, even for the most disciplined civil listener.

REFERENCES

Bakhtin, M. M. (1986). *Speech genres and other late essays.* Translated by V. W. McGee. Austin, TX: University of Texas.

Baxter, L. A., & Montgomery, B. W. (1996). *Relating: Dialogue and dialectics.* Mahwah, NJ: Lawrence Erlbaum.

Bolton, R. (1979). *Listening is more than merely hearing. People skills: How to assert yourself, listen to others, and resolve conflicts* (p. 51). Englewood Cliffs, NJ: Prentice-Hall.

Brooks, W. D., & Emmert, P. (1976) *Interpersonal communication.* Dubuque, IA: Wm. C. Brown.

Clark, K. B. (1980). Empathy: A neglected topic in psychological research. *American Psychologist, 35*(2): 187-190.

Howell, W. S. (1982). *The empathic communicator.* Belmont, CA: Wadsworth.

Jensen, J. V. (1981). *Argumentation: Reasoning in communication.* New York, NY: Van Nostrand Reinhold.

Katz, A. M., & Shotter, J. (1998). 'Living moments' in dialogical exchanges. *Human Systems, 9*: 81–93.

Merleau-Ponty, M. (1962). *Phenomenology of perception.* Translated by C. Smith. London, UK: Routledge and Kegan Paul.

Mutz, D. (2006). *Hearing the other side: Deliberative versus participative democracy.* New York, NY: Cambridge University Press.

Nichols, R. G., & Stevens, L. A. (1957). *Are you listening?* New York, NY: McGraw-Hill.

Olson, C. D., Genette, J., & Linde, J. (2013). Is civility lost forever? The impact of Civil Dialogue for citizens watching the 2012 presidential and vice presidential debates. Washington, DC: National Communication Association Convention.

Rogers, C. (1980). *A way of being.* Boston, MA: Houghton-Mifflin.

Shafir, R. Z. (2000). *The Zen of listening: Mindful communication in the age of distraction.* Wheaton, IL: Quest.

Shotter, J. (2009). Listening in a *way* that recognizes/realizes the world of 'the other'. *International Journal of Listening, 23*: 21–43.

Stauffer, J., Frost, R., & Rybolt, W. (1983). The attention factor in recalling network news. *Journal of Communication, 33*(1): 29–37.

Stewart, J., Zediker, K. E., & Witteborn, S. (2011). Empathic and dialogic listening. In J. Stewart (Ed.), *Bridges not walls: A book about interpersonal communication*, 11th ed. New York, NY: McGraw Hill.

Wittgenstein, L. (1980). *Culture and value.* Translated by P. Winch. Oxford, UK: Blackwell.

CHAPTER FIVE:
Creating a Civil Dialogue Event: The Necessary Framework

C ivil Dialogue can be used in multiple contexts to help people communicate in civil and productive ways, especially when they face "hot topics" and need to employ "cool heads." In a Civil Dialogue session, volunteer participants consider a provocative statement and have the opportunity to embody a position on the statement ranging from "Agree Strongly" to "Disagree Strongly." Participants are asked to follow guidelines for civility that are explained by the facilitator. The dialogue is then extended to the broader audience who are encouraged to respond with their own opinions and questions.

In this chapter, we provide practitioners a step-by-step explanation of a Civil Dialogue event. This includes a description of the Civil Dialogue format, suggestions for planning a Civil Dialogue event, an explanation of a Civil Dialogue round/session, and tips for creating a successful event. Samples of materials such as placards, programs, facilitator tracking sheets, and opening host statements are available at the Institute for Civil Dialogue website, www.civil-dialogue.com or in the appendices.

DESCRIPTION OF THE CIVIL DIALOGUE PLAYERS AND FORMAT

A Civil Dialogue event features five volunteer speakers in a structured discussion conducted by a facilitator in front of an audience. The speakers are chosen from the audience. If possible, it is helpful to support the facilitator with a host and an information source. The host welcomes the audience, introduces the facilitator at the start of the event, and serves as house manager during the event, monitoring the audience so the facilitator can focus on the dialogue. The information source acts as a resource to the facilitator (not to the speakers or audience directly), searching the Internet in real time as questions arise during the dialogue which may stymie the dialogue.

Using the Internet to check for factual information is not foolproof; some websites are not reliable, and it's difficult to verify the veracity of the source in real time. For this reason, we recommend that the information source (if called upon by the facilitator to conduct a search and subsequently announce any findings) report the source of the information as well as the findings. For example, "According to the *Wall Street Journal*…" or "The Congressional Budget Office website states… ." We recall one occasion, with regard to the potential impact of an immigration law in Arizona, where our information source found two contradictory forecasts from two think tanks with opposite ideologies. We reported both, demonstrating that even those who have studied the facts didn't agree, a discovery that emboldened our volunteer speakers.

It is also important to note that "facts" can be elusive. Consider this experiment conducted by Dan Ariely (2009), measuring the tendency to distrust facts when those facts have been "branded":

> [We] wanted to find out the degree to which people would doubt obviously truthful statements when these statements were associated with a brand. We started out by asking people whether they thought that completely unambiguous statements such as "the sun is yellow" and "a camel is bigger than a dog" were true or false, and 100 percent of the participants agreed they were true. Then we asked another group of people to evaluate the same statements, with the added information that they were made by either Proctor & Gamble, the Democratic Party, or the Republican Party. Would giving these statements a corporate or political origin color our participants' impressions and would they be more likely to suspect the truthfulness of these statements? The sad answer was yes. When we suggested that, say, the Democratic Party had issued the statement that "the sun is yellow," our participants were more likely to question it. ("Sure it's yellow, but it also has red spots on the surface and sometimes it looks white, so is it really just yellow?") If the Republican Party or P&G issued the statement that "a camel is bigger than a dog," the participants again were less certain and hedged their bets. ("What if the dog is a bull mastiff and the camel is a newborn . . . ?") By starting from a highly suspicious point of view, owing to the origin of the statement, the level of distrust was so high that it even influenced our participants' ability to identify obviously correct statements (259).

Ariely's conclusion underscores the reason why Civil Dialogue is focused on participants' positions and experiences, not facts. That being said, and despite the aforementioned risks involved in fact checking in real time, we believe fact checking is worthwhile if for no other reason than the mere presence of an information source can help thwart the impulse to make wild claims of "the earth is flat" variety.

Setting. A Civil Dialogue event can take place in a variety of settings, from classrooms to small theatres to living rooms. The room should be arranged into an "audience" area and a "stage" area with six chairs—five chairs for volunteer speakers who will be chosen from the audience and one chair for the facilitator. The five speaker chairs are set in a tight semicircle so that the speakers are in a position to talk to each other as well as to the facilitator and to the audience within a conversational distance. The facilitator's chair is placed at the open end of the semicircle, facing the five speakers. The information source should be placed in close proximity to the speaker and facilitator. The host should be in a position to monitor the audience and communicate to the facilitator and/or information source if needed.

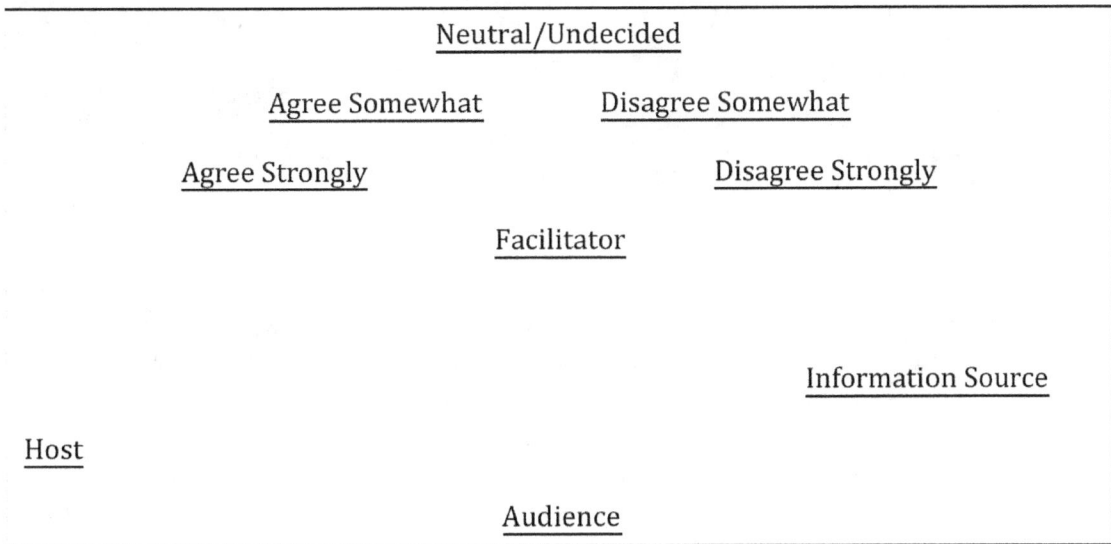

Neutral/Undecided

Agree Somewhat   Disagree Somewhat

Agree Strongly   Disagree Strongly

Facilitator

Information Source

Host

Audience

It is helpful to have fully visible placards on the chairs or behind the chairs on fully extended music stands to help the audience identify each position throughout a round of dialogue. It can also be helpful to print the placards two-sided to allow volunteer speakers a choice. "Neutral" and "Undecided," for example, both fall in the center of the agree–disagree spectrum, but they are subtly different positions. Printing "Neutral" on one side of the placard and "Undecided" on the other gives participants an opportunity to specify one position or the other. Also, it is sometimes a challenge to find participants who are willing to engage the dialogue from an extreme position. Making the "Strongly Agree" and "Strongly Disagree" placard reversible, with the other side marked simply "Agree" or "Disagree," might encourage participation. If placards are not available, the facilitator can define the chairs accordingly as potential speakers identify the positions they would be willing to take.

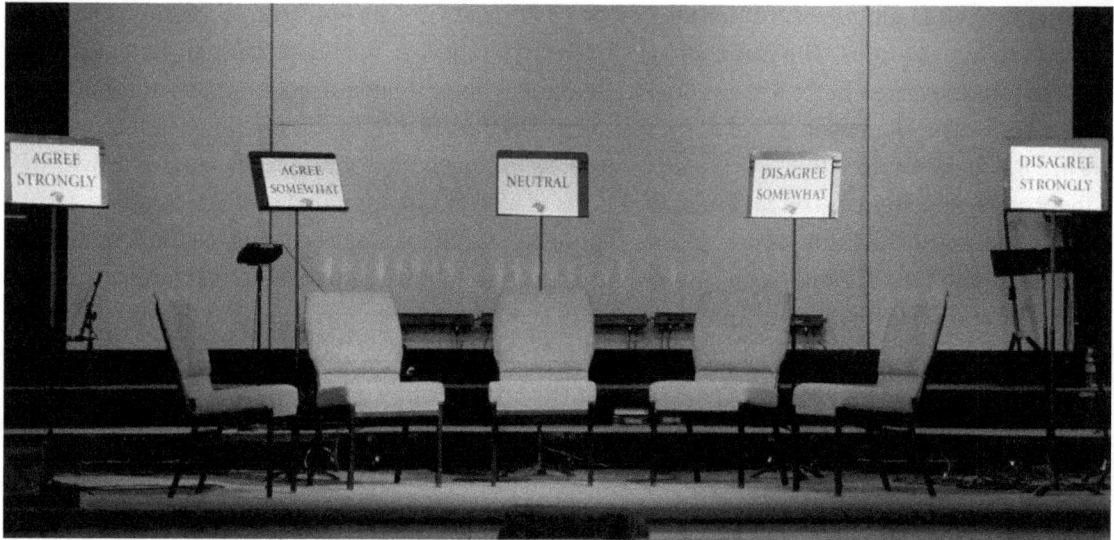

Pre-show. A pre-show is not required, but audiences have responded positively to pre-show PowerPoint displays of quotes about democracy and dialogue from politicians, civic leaders, and satirists, both historical and contemporary. Additionally, you may want to offer audiences a slide show with general information about the topic of the Civil Dialogue event so that they feel more prepared and invested. However, we caution against presenting too much material in advance of what is designed to be a spontaneous conversation. If you were to present well-articulated opinions from pundits, for example, the volunteer speakers might be tempted to regurgitate these previously developed opinions rather than speak extemporaneously based on how they felt about the issue and how much they knew about it when they walked into the room. Think about the state of mind a voter is in when walking into a voting booth; there is no further opportunity for study, but there is a meaningful opportunity to take a stand, and the moment is now.

Program/handout. Providing a printed program or handout can be helpful in a number of ways. It can provide audience members a place to take notes during a session of Civil Dialogue (we recommend having pencils available), it can offer an outline of the sequence of steps that take place in each round of Civil Dialogue, note the ground rules for civility, and it can provide suggested reading, links, and/or follow-up action items that encourage dialogue beyond having attended a session of Civil Dialogue. We do not recommend that the printed program include the exact wording of the statement(s) to be discussed; it is better to use a general topic such as "Reacting to the Presidential Debate." Keeping the printed program vague will help prevent audience members from getting ahead of the facilitator and pre-planning an argument.

PLANNING A CIVIL DIALOGUE EVENT

Ideally, a Civil Dialogue event utilizes a minimum of three organizers who can participate as host/house manager, facilitator, and information source. This team should work together closely prior to the event to craft or locate "hot topic" statements and conduct thorough research. All members of the team should be trained in the Civil Dialogue process, knowledgeable of the Civil Dialogue topic for the event, and familiar with the organization or group that is sponsoring the event.

When choosing a statement to consider, the Civil Dialogue team should pick strongly worded, one-sided, declarative statements. A Civil Dialogue event is intended to explore the most polarizing issues of our time and strongly worded statements are the most effective. Statements can be direct quotations from media sources or original statements crafted by the Civil Dialogue organizers. Avoid using lengthy and wordy statements because participants might get trapped in a discussion of semantics and not the topic itself. We typically draft and scrutinize our statements as a team in order to produce a good-quality statement that can strongly engage an audience in discussion.

Choosing a location for the Civil Dialogue event is easy, because the format is intended to be used in a variety of contexts and locales. No matter where a Civil Dialogue event is conducted, seating arrangements and acoustics should be considered so that everyone is able to fully participate in the dialogue. It is often useful to have an elevated stage for the dialogue itself or a raked seating arrangement for the audience. In most instances, we do not recommend video or audio taping the Civil Dialogue event. While such documentation of a session might be useful, the very presence of recording devices may alter the safe environment that Civil Dialogue advocates as essential to civil communication. Consider positioning these restrictions as a celebration of face-to-face interaction rather than a rebuke of technology.

A CIVIL DIALOGUE ROUND/EVENT

A round of Civil Dialogue typically lasts 30 to 40 minutes. In some settings, such as in a classroom setting that meets for less than an hour, time may only allow for one round. Public events often consist of two or even three rounds of Civil Dialogue. The following outline provides the process and timeline for a Civil Dialogue event:

- The host introduces the event. (5 minutes)

- Welcomes the audience and introduces the goals of a Civil Dialogue session.

  - Goal 1: To explore "hot topics" with "cool heads."

  - Goal 2: To honor all points of view without demonizing.

  - Goal 3: To foster participation in civil communication.

  - How Civil Dialogue works: Consider a statement, volunteers from the audience to fill the five chairs, elements of a round (as listed in the program).

  - Introduces the information source and explains his/her role.

  - Introduces the facilitator.

- The facilitator introduces the ground rules of civility.

  - By agreeing to these communication guidelines, we create a safer place for dialogue.

    - Participants can be passionate but not hostile.

    - Focus on how the statement makes you *feel*; you don't have to be an expert to have an opinion.

    - Avoid framing the dialogue as an argument to be won or lost.

  - Participants should use truthful speech that does not attack others.

    - "I" language shows conviction; "You" language implies critique.

    - Use your own words and avoid slogans that advocate your position.

    - Disagree without demonizing.

  - Participants should listen respectfully while others speak.

    - Listen with empathy rather than criticism.

    - Listen patiently; do not interrupt.

    - Do not engage in fake listening as you plan out what you want to say next.

- The facilitator reveals the provocative statement. (2–3 minutes)

  - Allows the audience to ponder the statement.

  - Offers clarification/discussion of terms in the statement.

  - Potentially offers historical or other pertinent information about the statement.

  - Calls for volunteer speakers to embody their position in the semicircle of five chairs.

- The facilitator prepares the speakers for the dialogue. (2–3 minutes)

  - Asks speakers to state their names.

  - Briefly confirms that the speakers understand the ground rules.

  - Chooses the order for the opening statements ("Linda, you were quick to take the 'Strongly Disagree' chair, so let's start with you.").

- Each speaker offers an opening statement. (5 minutes: approximately 1 minute each)

- The core dialogue. (10–15 minutes)

  - The five speakers talk to each other with minimal interruption.

  - The facilitator can call for a fact check from the information source.

  - The facilitator may need to intervene to ask questions, encourage clarification of statements, or diffuse a combative situation or open the dialogue for quieter members.

- The dialogue is opened to the audience. (5–10 minutes)

  - The facilitator invites audience questions/comments.

  - The five speakers are not excluded from this interaction.

- The facilitator returns to the speakers to closes the round. (5 minutes)

  - Speakers offer closing statements, often in the reverse order of the opening statements. (1 minute each)

  - Speakers are thanked and return to their seats.

- A wrap-up summary/statement is offered by the facilitator.

  - If another round is pending, the facilitator reveals the statement to be examined, then calls for a short break.

  - If the session has concluded, the facilitator turns the event back to the host.

- The host closes the event.

  - Encourages feedback from the audience through survey/email.

  - Directs the audience to additional resources on the topic.

TIPS TO CREATE A SUCCESSFUL CIVIL DIALOGUE EVENT

Our experience suggests that the ideal running time for a Civil Dialogue event appears to be about 90 minutes without an intermission. If audience members are eager to participate, it is possible to stage three rounds in that amount of time. However, there are times when the facilitator may need to employ the pedagogic tool known as "wait time," particularly in the first round, creating a comfortable atmosphere and giving participants an extra moment or two to bring themselves to volunteer as speakers. Similarly, during a round of Civil Dialogue, some participants may need to be prodded, cajoled, or encouraged. At times, it may be necessary to ask if someone would be willing to explore what it would be like to occupy a certain chair, even if one's own beliefs differ. If these conditions arise, experience shows that it is better to let the round play out in a more expansive way, even if it means that the event has to be limited to two rounds. Often we have limited a Civil Dialogue event to two rounds and then allowed attendees of the event to spend the remaining time talking informally with one another about the topic and the Civil Dialogue format.

REFERENCE

Ariely, Dan (2009). *Predictably irrational, revised and expanded edition: The hidden forces that shape our decisions*. HarperCollins e-books. Kindle Edition.

CHAPTER SIX:
The Role of the Audience in Civil Dialogue

Herbert Blau (1990) reminds us that "gathered in the audience are issues of representation, repression, otherness, the politics of the unconscious, ideology, and power" (p. 26). Blau's statement about theatrical audiences deepens our understanding of Civil Dialogue audiences by reminding us that they are likely comprised of complicated human beings who operate both as individual agents and as a collective group. Civil Dialogue events are advertised as a place where all opinions are welcome and people typically attend the events because they hold an interest in the topic being discussed or as a way to learn more about civil communication. Not all people who attend Civil Dialogue events choose to speak, yet their contributions to the process as audience members are overwhelmingly significant. We offer this discussion of the audience component of the Civil Dialogue format as a way of understanding the impact that an audience can have on civil communication and to feature the role it plays in the success of the Civil Dialogue format. We organize our discussion of the Civil Dialogue audience into three categories: the *general audience* that initially arrives at the Civil Dialogue event, the *dialogue audience* that emerges within and among the core dialogue with the five volunteers, and the *spectator audience* comprised of the Civil Dialogue participants who watch the core dialogue.

THE GENERAL AUDIENCE: WHO ATTENDS A CIVIL DIALOGUE?

Park-Fuller (2003) notes that there are limitations and challenges associated with fully understanding the audience experience. Civil Dialogue meets this challenge in the way we promote the format as mobile and accessible. We have staged Civil Dialogue events in large and small theatre spaces, university classrooms, museums, community centers, and at conferences and places of worship. We have determined that the physical location for the Civil Dialogue has little impact on the participation levels from the audience. Large audiences of over 100 have engaged the format with great energy and enthusiasm, hands raised, eager to have their moment at the microphone. Smaller audiences of 10 or less have taken on a collective quality of intimacy and rich analysis of the provocative statement. These smaller audiences often delve deeply into the topic presented and feel at ease disclosing their own stories and experiences with it. The structure of the format allows for a balanced approach to participation for audiences (large or small) and they play a key role in the generation of information that the overall Civil Dialogue event produces.

In a world of increasing hostility and incivility, it is a challenge for members of society to find productive places to talk with one another. Putnam (2000) argues that American society needs an infinite variety of informal ties to link to one another. He comments that over the last third of the 20th century we have been pulled apart from one another and our communities. Sennett (2012) describes the United States as an intensely tribal society and argues that "tribalism couples solidarity with others like yourself to aggression against those who differ" (p. 4). With this as the reality of our American culture, we are encouraged that people who come to Civil Dialogue events and make up our general audiences are working toward what Sennett refers to as a demanding and difficult kind of cooperation (p. 6). It is essential that audiences in Civil Dialogues represent varying viewpoints that cross the spectrum of the provocative statement. This cooperation "tries to join people who have separate or conflicting interests, who do not feel good about each other, who are unequal, or who simply do not understand one another" (p. 6). Barber (1984) makes a case for transformation via a product of conflict rather than consensus within communities. He argues, "Local public or small-scale private activity seems to be vital to civil education in . . .modern democracy" (p. 234). He boldly states, "Without talk, there can be no democracy" (p. 267). We believe that the gathering of people in public spaces to talk about difficult topics has the capacity to diminish the negative effects of American nationalism. The general audience is comprised of people willing to risk dialogue and disagreement and understand there is much to be gained from understanding the differences they have with others.

The notion of having a public audience is key to the success of Civil Dialogue. The very fact that an audience witnesses and, in essence, holds participants accountable for their statements is crucial. In a world where facts are suspect and people often make decisions based on feelings alone, having speakers held accountable by an audience for the statements they make in public encourages honesty and discourages the fictionalization of facts. Indeed, as Aristotle first suggested, an audience holds a speaker accountable for his/her words (Frank, 2015). This means that the "public" nature of Civil Dialogue is crucial. The very fact that all speakers are responsible for their remarks in front of a live audience discourages them from creating facts, fictionalizing accounts, exaggerating claims, or positioning themselves in perspectives where audience members may knowingly contradict the grounds of their argument. Merely the presence of a live audience who have the potential to point out the erroneous nature of their claims discourages such actions, particularly in a public setting.

We are often asked why we do not present Civil Dialogue in the digital realm: filming events so they can be posted online for subsequent commentary, or live-streaming a video so an online audience can contribute comments and questions via Twitter, etc. We resist this because (1) we believe the immediacy of an audience increases the integrity of the dialogue and (2) the inclusion of a digital audience would change the nature of the in-person dynamic and could make the setting more intimidating for participants not comfortable being videotaped/live-streamed. Some of the most egregious examples of incivility and hate are played out in the digital realm where perceptions of anonymity fuel uncivil communication. Again, we make reference to our own scholarship (Mckinnon, 2012) as published in *USA Today,* where our efforts to create civility were belittled by readers who could comment anonymously. The Civil Dialogue audience meets in a face-to-face setting, physical bodies in one space together, with the understanding that other human beings will be affected by what they say and do.

THE DIALOGUE AUDIENCE: WHAT HAPPENS WHEN SOMEONE TAKES A CHAIR?

The staging of Civil Dialogue is inspired in part by Augusto Boal (1995), creator of the Theatre of the Oppressed, Forum Theatre, and Legislative Theatre. Carlson (1999) explains that, for Boal, "art merged with daily activity" as "a means of exploring social situations and of developing leadership and coping skills in the participant/audience" (p. 120). Much of Boal's work focused on a reimagining of audience as shareholders rather than passive observers. He believed that empowerment happened when people moved from passive witnessing to active speaking. Pelias and VanOosting (1987) provide a similar model for audience participation, naming audiences as receivers, respondents, coproducers, and producers (p. 226), depending on the degree of their participation. Conceptualizing audiences as coproducing and producing allows us to shift our understanding of audience away from passivity and provides for audience contributions such as those made by people in the Civil Dialogue core dialogue. It is at this site of participation that we see the potential for Civil Dialogue as an opportunity for audience experience. In his discussion of performance ethnography, Conquergood (1985) writes about the moral complexity of responding to the "other" and names genuine conversation as a "dialogic performance" (p. 4). The five core participants in a round of Civil Dialogue work to cocreate a genuine and civil conversation through dialogic exchanges. To do this, they must audience one another closely and work to follow ground rules for civil listening presented to them at the beginning of the dialogue. As discussed in Chapter Four, civil listening is a highly dynamic process that involves being engaged, brave, and respectful. A participant must expect a level of interaction from others that meets the level that they are exerting. We have observed that Civil Dialogue core participants monitor one another's communication and remind each other of the purpose of Civil Dialogue. As facilitators, we often hold back on intervening if ground rules are not followed, knowing that participants often notice these infractions and will find ways to both highlight and correct the problem. In this sense, the dialogue audience becomes a corrective audience, modeling civil communication—indeed, demanding it of the other participants.

Dialogue audiences are frequently exposed to the sharing of personal narratives during the core dialogue because it is common for core dialogue participants to explain their positions on "hot topics" through the telling of personal stories and anecdotes. When this happens, the dialogue audience may experience what Alexander (2000) refers to as audience reflexivity, or the capacity for perceptive audience members to "turn, bend, or reflect back upon their own lived experiences" (p. 101). In his theory of generative autobiography, Alexander describes the ways that an audience experiences a subjective connection with the storyteller which allows for a larger sociopolitical context of sharing. The locus of control remains with the audience as they determine which part of the story being told has saliency to their own beliefs and positions. The core dialogue participants are also in a dialogic exchange with the members of the spectator audience who are watching them. Volunteers who have taken a chair have remarked that the presence of the spectator audience has a significant impact on their awareness of their verbal and nonverbal communication. The dialogue audience is provided with a reminder that they are being asked to communicate within a structure of civility with ground rules and they are held responsible for the ways that they speak, listen, and embody the position they have taken.

In the early years of Civil Dialogue, we experimented with having a more interactive exchange between the dialogue audience and spectator audience and by allowing "lifelines," borrowed from a popular television gameshow. Spectator audience members who agreed with a certain speaker could hand a supportive note to a runner who would deliver it to the speaker during the dialogue. We discovered that this interrupted the dialogue too much because speakers could not listen to others when reading notes. Another tactic was to allow a second "shadow" speaker to stand behind and support the participant who had volunteered for a chair. In both instances, the integrity of the civil exchange was compromised by the interruption. Additionally, we have monitored spectator audience influence on the core dialogue by requesting that they observe the core dialogue respectfully until it is their opportunity to join the dialogue. In some instances, the facilitator has had to intervene and monitor the spectator audience's responses (mostly nonverbal in the form of sighs, rolling of eyes, and intentional shifts of the body to make a point). We have found it important to constrain audience participation throughout the various stages of the Civil Dialogue process.

THE SPECTATOR AUDIENCE: WHO IS WATCHING A CIVIL DIALOGUE?

The spectator audience of a Civil Dialogue takes many forms and has the potential to have a significant impact on the Civil Dialogue event. The collective group shares the role of audience as the facilitator unveils the provocative statement and provides a context for the core dialogue. Once volunteers move to their chosen positions to begin the core dialogue, the general audience now shifts to a role of critical observer of the information exchanged in the core dialogue. Since the provocative statement has likely generated a response from audience members ranging from "Strongly Agree" to "Strongly Disagree," they are not intellectually "passive" as the core dialogue begins. The active audience position could mean that Civil Dialogue audiences work to create a certain amount of distance from the words of dialogue participants with whom they disagree. This phenomenon is similar to Bertolt Brecht's notion of alienation where audiences obtain critical consciousness by not empathizing or connecting with the words/experiences of the performance they are watching (Bell, 2008). Bell compares the Brechtian framing of audience as a critically conscious observer to Aristotle's description of the audience as spectator, delegating power to the performer to think for them, thereby creating an experience of catharsis (p. 207). When we analyze the Civil Dialogue audience using an Aristotelian approach, we might imagine that the core dialogue, when the five participants are speaking exclusively to one another, allows for the spectator audience to delegate their response to provocation to the speakers and experience a wide range of possible emotional catharsis from agreement to anger, even fear. The passionate statements made by the "Strongly Agree" or "Disagree" chairs are often delivered with intensity and conviction. Since many people are cautious, even fearful, to engage in public disagreement with others, an ability to be an audience member in a more passive role might productively function as a cathartic experience. Audience members might hear the words they actually believe and think, but cannot voice themselves, spoken aloud by others in the context of the dialogue or even during the audience participation phase.

When the facilitator moves from the core dialogue and opens the discussion to the entire audience, the spectator audience shifts his or her role once again, and now becomes a more active shareholder—similar to Boal's reimagining of participatory audiences. Those who attend Civil Dialogue events regularly remark that they look forward to the audience participation segment, because it is a time for them to contribute to the information that is disseminated during the core dialogue. Audience members often ask questions, support the positions represented by the core participants through their own stories and knowledge sharing, or even challenge the dialogue participants to reframe or reengage the ideas that they have spoken about to one another.

As noted, it is difficult to truly gauge the experience of an audience. Our interactions with audiences over the years have shown us that audiences are powerful entities in the Civil Dialogue format and that add great depth to the civil communication process. Through the various means of audience participation we understand the critical roles that a Civil Dialogue audience plays in hopes that it provides a richer understanding of this important component of our format.

REFERENCES

Alexander, B. (2000) Skin flint (or, the garbage man's kid): A generative autobiographical performance based on Tami Spry's tattoo stories. *Text and Performance Quarterly, 20*: 1, 97–114.

Barber, B. R. (1984). *Strong democracy, participatory politics for a new age.* Berkeley, CA: University of California Press.

Bell, E. (2008). *Theories of performance.* Los Angeles, CA: Sage.

Blau, H. (1990). *The audience.* London, UK: The Johns Hopkins University Press.

Boal, A. (1995). *The rainbow of desire: The Boal method of theatre and therapy.* London, UK: Routledge.

Carlson, M. (1999). *Performance: A critical introduction.* New York, NY: Routledge.

Conquergood, D. (1985). Performing as a moral act: Ethical dimensions of the ethnography of performance. *Literature in Performance, 5*: 1–13.

Frank, J. (2015). On *logos* and politics in Aristotle. In R. Lockwood and T. Samara (Eds.), *Aristotle's politics: A critical guide.* Cambridge, UK: Cambridge University Press.

Mckinnon, S. (2012). After Giffords shooting, civility still elusive. *USA Today* (January 6): 1.

Park-Fuller, L. (2003). Audiencing the audience: Playback theatre, performative writing, and social activism. *Text and Performance Quarterly, 23*(3): 288–310.

Pelias, R., & VanOosting, J. (1987). A paradigm for performance studies. *Quarterly Journal of Speech, 73*: 219–231.

Putnam, R. D. (2000). *Bowling alone: The collapse and revival of American community.* New York, NY: Simon & Schuster.

Sennett, R. (2012). *Together: The rituals, pleasures and politics of co-operation.* London, UK: Yale University Press.

CHAPTER SEVEN:
The Art of Facilitation

The word *facilitate* comes from the Latin term *facilis* or *facile*, which means "to render easy" or "make easier." This term was a conscious choice over *moderator, leader,* or any of a variety of terms that could have been chosen, because in Civil Dialogue, a facilitator should help make conversation among the participants and audience members easy. This does not discount the multiplicity of roles that the facilitator must play as indeed the role undoubtedly includes a plethora of skills. A good facilitator is part therapist, attentive listener, encourager of those less vocal, and balancer of turn taking (ensuring no one participant monopolizes the conversation). The person models civil communication skills needed to create a successful dialogue, serves as timekeeper, and provides the ultimate summary of what themes and lessons have arisen from the dialogue.

The role of a successful facilitator may also include the task of hosting the dialogue, though that can be separated out if there are adequate trained people leading the dialogue. Initially a host welcomes the participants to the dialogue, provides a brief history of Civil Dialogue, explains the process and rules of Civil Dialogue, and then introduces the facilitator. If just one person is performing all roles, the host may transition directly into the role of facilitator. A sample host statement is provided in Appendix E.

CHOOSING THE STATEMENT

A round of Civil Dialogue begins with a provocative statement. Madison (2005) suggests that to be provocative allows for an unsettling of the taken-for-granted and can lead us to critical awareness. She articulates provocation as a way to generate memories that we may not otherwise recall. The statement is designed to provoke curiosity and push participants to evaluate their position on a particular topic. Initially, the facilitator has the responsibility for selecting the final topic and choosing the wording of the provocative statement. This alone is a significant task as the topic must be "hot" enough to have ground on both sides of the agree–disagree continuum. A statement should not be worded so that the majority of the audience would likely be partial to one side or the other, but should be captivating enough and thoughtful to promote an interesting discussion. From the inception of Civil Dialogue, quotations were chosen, frequently from known politicians, so the credibility of the source would often weigh into the conversation. Quotations have the advantage of removing the responsibility of any perceived bias from the facilitator and are often good starting places for discussion. However, for the very reason they may be successful, it is also possible that the person making the statement may become the focus of the dialogue instead of the context of the quotation. Hence it may be worthwhile to craft a well-worded statement after doing extensive reading on a topic. Again, the wording should ensure that both sides have equivalent ground and the terms chosen should be easily understood by the audience, not include "loaded" language that may provoke multiple interpretations, and a single word should not appear as the focus of the statement. Crafting the language of the statement carefully improves the focus of the dialogue and guards against participants getting sidetracked and attacking the linguistic choices or hijacking the dialogue by focusing on a single term which they may find prejudicial or problematic. We often work as a team to write the provocative statement; however, the final wording of the statement should be the purview of the facilitator as he or she will be the one moderating the discussion and providing the necessary background for the audience before filling the chairs. The wording of sample topics previously used is included in Appendix B.

The facilitator is responsible for presenting information to the Civil Dialogue participants that explains and introduces the general topic but does not reveal the provocative statement in advance. This can be done in a pre-show presentation that features multiple perspectives on the topic, including quotations, videos, and even performance/art-based explanations.

ORIENTING THE AUDIENCE TO THE STATEMENT

Once the topic has been revealed, it is often helpful for the facilitator to provide useful background material, a short history of the controversy, and to go over the wording of the statement to ensure that all audience members understand the nature of the statement. During this explanation, participants have the time to consider whether they may agree/disagree with the statement and to what degree they hold their feelings. The facilitator can direct the audience to the program so that they can record the statement and their position. A sample program can be found in Appendix C. Often it is wise for the facilitator to briefly recap the rules of Civil Dialogue and to review the process to ensure that audience members will feel comfortable assuming a chair. To aid in the progress of the dialogue, we have crafted a tracking sheet on which the facilitator can take notes to assist in the process of making the dialogue easy and balanced for both participants and audience members. A sample tracking sheet can be found in Appendix F.

SELECTING PARTICIPANTS

Perhaps one of the most challenging tasks of the facilitator is to fill the chairs. Once the statement has been revealed and explained, the facilitator can open up the staging area for participants to assume a chair. Depending on the audience, some chairs may be immediately filled by members who strongly hold positions and are not reticent to share their opinions. If the chairs do not quickly fill, it is the job of the facilitator to perhaps coax interested audience members to become willing to share their opinions. This is what we call "wait time." Wait time can often test the patience of a facilitator who is eager to begin the dialogue. However, we find it useful to provide sufficient wait time so that potential participants do not misinterpret a statement, or assume a chair which comprises a position they don't believe, or feel a sense of obligation to fill a chair. During wait time, the facilitator can provide additional choices for taking a position. Since each chair can be modified, the facilitator can extend position options to the audience. For example, the "Strongly Disagree" placard can be turned around to reveal "Disagree," which may be a more accurate position for a potential participant. If nearly all chairs have been filled and there seems to be no one who strongly identifies with the remaining chair(s), the facilitator may ask if anyone would be willing to assume a certain position or chair that has not yet been filled. We find it best that if someone is taking a position that they don't fully believe that they self-identify as such so as not to violate the integrity of the dialogue. Filling the chairs is a duty incumbent upon the facilitator and the success of the dialogue truly depends upon the participants chosen to assume the chairs.

BEGINNING THE DIALOGUE

Once the chairs are filled, the facilitator also assumes a chair facing the participants with his or her back to the audience. The facilitator begins by asking the names of the participants and refers to their name in conjunction with the position they have chosen. Frequent repetition of the names helps familiarize the audience with the participants. Writing the participants' names on the tracking sheet also helps the facilitator recall the names during the dialogue. Use of name tags is also a helpful way to make participants feel comfortable when beginning a dialogue.

When participants arrive in the room where the dialogue is to be held, we frequently ask them to complete name tags, as it makes it easier to identify people, both those who participate by taking a chair, or as a member of the audience. The structure of Civil Dialogue purposely does not provide for introductions other than name, as credentialing can occur which can affect the power dynamic of the group as well as the flow of interaction (Olson, 1986). If any member of the dialogue is perceived to have greater expertise than others, it can shut down the free flow of ideas and inhibit participants' willingness to contribute. If credentials do become evident during the dialogue, it's usually as part of an individual's narrative and has more meaning in that context than serving as an introduction of panelists.

After the names have been repeated, the facilitator asks for the participants to make their 1-minute statements as to why they have chosen the chair they did or a brief history of their personal feelings about the statement. These statements become the starting ground for the dialogue so we find it useful to frequently begin with the side "Agree"/"Disagree" where the first chair was taken as often they hold the most ardent viewpoint. The facilitator must ensure that these statements are clearly understood and may frequently need to ask follow-up questions to clarify the positions of people who may not provide an easily understood rationale for why they took a chair. The facilitator should also ensure that all five statements are roughly equal in time. From our experience we have found that people have very differing concepts about what constitutes a minute. Therefore, the presence of a stopwatch or some larger timekeeping device that may even be in the view of the audience can help equalize or balance these opening statements. Once everyone has had the opportunity to make their introductory remarks, the facilitator leaves his or her chair and physically moves away from the five participants in the dialogue, shifting to the side or behind the participants to a place where he or she can monitor the dialogue without being in line of the participants' comments, thus not assuming a leadership role in the dialogue. This movement encourages the five participants to have a dialogue without having to raise hands for turn taking or to seek permission from the facilitator. The dialogue is then monitored from a short distance. We do not recommend that the facilitator join the larger audience, rather they should maintain a close proximity to the core dialogue participants. The facilitator can take notes on what comments they find particularly insightful or significant. Additionally, they can chart the number of turns each participant takes to try to ensure a balanced dialogue. If the dialogue bogs down or becomes unclear, the facilitator may provide suggestions for how the dialogue can progress. Again, if some statement is particularly unclear, the facilitator may request clarification from a participant. If a certain participant doesn't speak, the facilitator can call upon that person either by name or position to share his or her viewpoints. Likewise, the facilitator may need to summarize or concisely restate a position if one person presents a complex or compound idea. Since the nature of Civil Dialogue is to have people spontaneously share their opinions, the lack of planning often yields people thinking on their feet, testing the wording of their ideas, and merely talking through how they might feel. It is the task of the facilitator to aid in this process by ensuring that all thoughts are recognized, legitimized, and comprehended by all. Here is where a facilitator's active listening skills are often tested, as the facilitator has to make a judgment call about when to interject comments, clarify, and/or support the participants. If a particular person is being challenged or made to feel threatened, typically assuming a physical presence behind that person's chair can offer support and help shield the person from attack. Ultimately, again, the facilitator must determine when approximately 10 to 15 minutes have elapsed and find an appropriate time when either the discussion has become repetitive or that the five participants have had sufficient opportunity to air their views and it is time to bring the audience into the dialogue.

MONITORING AUDIENCE PARTICIPATION

The next phase of the Civil Dialogue is to include the remaining audience members in the discussion. While monitoring the comments made by the dialogue participants during the first portion of the Civil Dialogue, it is also incumbent upon the facilitator to be astutely aware of the audience and their feelings. The larger the audience the more likely there are to be side conversations among members, feeling the need to express their opinions. The facilitator must be sensitive to these "rumblings" and be sure to include audience members before their frustration level becomes too high. Once the facilitator has stopped the dialogue from the participants in the chairs, he or she can call on audience members to provide their opinions and feelings, to state their positions, or to merely ask questions of the panelists. Again, the facilitator should be sure to monitor this phase for balanced viewpoints, trying to call for opposing viewpoints from the audience if one side seems to be getting too much "air time." This portion of the dialogue should take approximately 10 to 15 minutes but may be extended if the audience is large and there seems to be plenty of new information contributed to the dialogue. Likewise, if there is only a single Civil Dialogue occurring, this phase may run longer than normal to accommodate and help audience members feel like their viewpoint was heard and their participation valued. Again, the facilitator should be listing significant contributions made by the audience on their tracking sheet for later reference when closing the round. Once the facilitator has determined that sufficient audience contributions have been made, they then return to the five original participants by physically rejoining the dialogue by assuming their original chair facing the panelists. With their back to the audience, it provides a nonverbal signal that attention should once again be given exclusively to the five dialogue participants.

INFORMATION SOURCE

At any point during the original dialogue and/or audience interaction, the facilitator may find it necessary to call on the role of an information source. For purposes of clarifying statements made, discovering facts which participants may recall, but not fully, or to intentionally correct comments which the facilitator knows are false, the facilitator can request the services of the information source, another person, perhaps the host, someone who is familiar with the topic area and has access to a computer to verify information given or find answers to particularly vexing questions which stymie the dialogue. Normally, the mere presence of an information source serves as a deterrent for people making unreasonable, prejudicial, or slanted viewpoints or incorrectly citing statistics. However, sometimes the lack of certain information may impede the progress of the dialogue and then the facilitator should feel free to call on the information source to find out what information can be found in a reasonable amount of time. Often the dialogue progresses without this information until the information source is able to provide the useful information. Even then, the information source should always provide the source of the data found so everyone can assess the credibility and potential bias of that source. Just as the facilitator works to provide an impartial view of the statement regardless of personal beliefs, the information source should likewise try to provide the most useful and least biased evidence when consulting Internet sources. If there is some document that the facilitator believes will often be referenced during the dialogue or some sources that were particularly helpful as the facilitator was doing background research, the facilitator may share that with the information source in advance so the researcher can knowingly be ready to consult those sources.

CLOSING THE DIALOGUE

Finally, once back in place with the participants, the facilitator calls for closing statements from each of the panelists, typically in the reverse order from the opening statements. The facilitator may choose to ask what issues that arose were most important, if the person would assume the same chair after participating in the dialogue, if viewpoints have strengthened in intensity or shifted, or just leave it open for whatever participants choose to say. Again, it is often easy for the most vocal participants to want to extensively summarize their opinions in an effort to sway other members to their viewpoint, at which time the facilitator may need to cut them off or remind them that the purpose of Civil Dialogue is not to gain adherence, but merely to achieve understanding. Having a timer visible often makes this task easier as the responsibility seems to shift from the facilitator to the clock and the facilitator merely needs to reference time to ensure fairness to all participants. Once all five participants have had the opportunity to speak, the facilitator announces that the round has been completed, thanks the participants by beginning a round of applause, and ushering participants to their seats so that only the facilitator remains in front.

SUMMARIZING THE DIALOGUE

To officially close the round of dialogue, the facilitator now must summarize and conclude the dialogue. Here is where the comments that were written on the tracking sheet often become handy. The facilitator typically does more than just recap the statements of the participants, but tries to draw some larger lessons that were learned or some recurring themes that arose during the Civil Dialogue. The facilitator may indicate what statements he or she found particularly interesting or begin by noting information learned during the dialogue. Another tact is to try to reference significant statements made by each participant to make each person feel like they made a worthwhile contribution to the dialogue. Perhaps just describing the process the dialogue took may be a sufficient closer. Whatever method the facilitator takes, all members should be left feeling that there was significant and meaningful progress made by virtue of witnessing and/or participating in the Civil Dialogue. In addition, references to examples of civil communication underscore the ability to model civility in action. In essence, this final summary is the bow the facilitator ties around the package to add a touch of beauty to the process.

FINDING YOUR STYLE OF FACILITATION

Undoubtedly each person who acts as a facilitator brings along a vast number of past experiences, education, and philosophy about how they approach the role of facilitator. While this chapter has elucidated what exact functions a facilitator of Civil Dialogue may find helpful, we acknowledge there are a variety of approaches to successful facilitation.

The styles of facilitation date back to early studies in psychology which identify three primary styles of leadership: authoritarian, democratic, and laissez-faire (Lewin, Lippitt, & White, 1939). While broadly used in research throughout the past century, it is important to note that these three styles tend to be confined by the conventions of a therapeutic setting and the inherent goals therein. As such, we mention them to offer perspectives which are often discussed when considering facilitation styles.

Authoritarian, or autocratic leadership is highly directive in nature. Facilitators take an active role as leader, delegating tasks to participants, watching to ensure that everyone fulfills their predesignated role. Often a highly directive facilitator is presumed to be an expert and one to whom group members and the audience look to for advice, approval, and adherence. While there is a given structure to Civil Dialogue, a facilitator with authoritarian characteristics may find more success in the role of "conductor," as in an orchestra. Musicians each play their own part, and a master conductor seeks to bring out the melodies and harmonies distinct to each instrument. Likewise in Civil Dialogue, autocratic facilitators may best find themselves only providing the structure for the dialogue, then allowing the various participants to create the melodies and harmonies of the dialogue, reasserting their leadership only when shifting from one movement to another (i.e., moving from the core dialogue to audience participation). Facilitators adhering to an authoritarian style may take their best advice from the Hippocratic oath: "First, do no harm."

Democratic facilitators seek the participation of all group members. While the notion of democracy implies an "election," it is rare to find an official election among democratic leaders who are not office-holders, but function largely as facilitators. Instead, as a descriptive term, the democratic facilitator solicits input from all members about their role and inquires how other participants might balance that role toward a mutual goal or purpose. In the context of Civil Dialogue, a democratic facilitator might inquire which of the participants in the core dialogue wishes to proceed first with the opening statement, moving in an order preferred by the participants in the dialogue as opposed to an order predetermined by the facilitator. When moving from the core dialogue to audience participation, a democratic facilitator might first check with the five participants to be sure they have said most of what they wanted to say before proceeding to interaction with the audience. Obviously, a democratic facilitator still needs to be aware of time constraints and to ensure that participation is roughly equal among members.

A laissez-faire facilitator provides minimal structure, allowing participants to lead themselves. While this "hands off" approach may initially sound like the easiest style of facilitation to adopt, it can, indeed, be the most difficult. Laissez-faire leadership has predominantly been used when training leaders and teams in a business setting using principles from Gestalt therapy. Bentley (1994) describes facilitation as the provision of opportunities, resources, encouragement, and support for the group to succeed in achieving its objectives, and to do this through enabling the group to take control and responsibility for the way they proceed. Laissez-faire facilitation is premised on the notion of trust and the recognition that the dialogue you facilitate is not your own. Heider (1986) admonishes facilitators to "[R]emember that you are facilitating another person's process. It is not your process. Do not instruct. Do not control. o not force your own needs and insights into the foreground. If you do not trust a person's process, that person will not trust you" (p. 17). In essence, laissez-faire facilitation is diametrically opposed to the authoritarian style. Bentley (1994) further describes the "process" of facilitation as also including nonaction, silence, and even the facilitator's absence.

As a technique of facilitation, Bentley (1994) suggests that open-ended questions are a facilitator's keys to opening the doors and windows into what is going on for the group and the individual members of the group. While anyone can ask a question, good facilitation is to know and to ask the right question as the right time. It is through questions that a facilitator can release the potential of the group, engendering a nonthreatening environment, creating trust, and demonstrating and accepting both mistakes (opportunities for growth) and successes. Adopting a laissez-faire facilitation style takes courage, much like participating in a Civil Dialogue.

During the past decade that we have developed the role of facilitator for Civil Dialogues, we have experimented with, tested, and adopted a wide variety of facilitator styles. Initially, the role of facilitator was conceived to fit along the lines of Boal's Theatre of the Oppressed, where the facilitator was a joker or trickster, to provide a counterweight to extreme ideas. As the concept of Civil Dialogue has evolved, we have assumed a more hands-off approach, concurring with Bentley (1994) when he suggested, "It puzzles people at first, to see how little the able leader actually does, and yet how much gets done" (p. 11). Our experiences of facilitation prove that often the best facilitation is to allow the participants to control the process. Time after time we've witnessed when a dialogue appears to be getting off track or away from the statement, the participants become self-correcting and it is their comments that return the dialogue to its focus. It is our belief that it is far better for the participants to recognize how they wish to explore the statement within the context of Civil Dialogue, and then gently nudge them toward that end.

FACILITATION SKILLS

Regardless of what facilitation style you may find most suited to you, there are some basic fundamental skills that can aid in the process of facilitation. Anderson and Robertson (1985) elucidate several skills which we find appropriate to the facilitation of Civil Dialogue. Initially, they suggest that the facilitator needs to actively attend to the dialogue. While we've discussed why mindfully following the dialogue is essential, providing eye contact, when appropriate, and demonstrating physical alertness are also critical keys. Eye contact can be a powerful monitoring tool when engaging in dialogue. Typically, whoever receives the bulk of the eye contact is perceived as having the most power. This is why during opening statements and especially during the core dialogue, the facilitator may not want to engage in direct eye contact with the speaker, so that comments will be directed toward the other participants and not toward the facilitator who, by virtue of the fact that he or she began the dialogue, is perceived to be in a position of authority.

Secondly, Anderson and Robertson (1985) advise a facilitator to communicate clearly, being able to successful paraphrase and summarize ideas which others may find confusing, interpreting without repeating or advantaging any one position. Here the key is to monitor your own commentary, being sure not to give more "air time" to a position with which you agree, through your own repetition or amplification. Self-censorship on the part of the facilitator is crucial to ensure that each position is weighted fairly during the dialogue.

Perhaps what is most essential is for the facilitator to model civil behavior. The facilitator is the one person everyone looks to for how to engage in civil communication, so that modeling the skills of a civil communicator, including the skill of civil listening, is tantamount to success.

For the facilitator, civil listening incurs the added burden of trying to link thoughts together thematically. While this can be done during the core dialogue, it is often a skill that occurs when summarizing the dialogue. A good facilitator helps the audience understand the progress that they've made, points to how they've enacted civility, and highlights what has been learned from the experience.

Smith (2000) has pointed to several specific techniques facilitators should be mindful of. He suggests initially being clear as to what one perceives is the role of the facilitator. We've presented a host of stylistic characteristic than a facilitator can embody. Knowing your own style and approach is essential if those you facilitate are to understand your perspective. Next, Smith suggests that facilitators provide a workable agenda and process. Given that the goal of Civil Dialogue is to model civility, typically a specific agenda is not essential, for as Bentley (1994) points out, it is easier to adapt to a process and to change without an agenda. This allows people to change their mind during the context of a dialogue, which is a concept key to civility. Managing the process and building trust are key ingredients to successful facilitation.

Toward this end, Smith (2000) suggests ample use of open-ended questions and asking people to summarize what might become a long train of thought. As some participants are working through their position(s) on an issue, asking them to pause and summarize what they've just said can serve as a strong reminder of their reasoning process.

Finally, Smith (2000) notes that the role of the facilitator is to keep people involved. Typically, this means staying out of the limelight, intervening only when necessary and maintaining absolute neutrality.

The role of the facilitator is a complex one. It is one that is improved with experience, and best when one can trust his or her own skills to achieve the best possible dialogue. A facilitator is not a leader; a facilitator is not a discussant or panelist; a facilitator is not a policy expert. Perhaps Smith (2000) summarizes the role best when he notes that a good facilitator is merely "a servant of the group" (p. 17).

REFERENCES

Anderson, L. F., & Robertson, S. E. (1985). Group facilitation: Functions and skills. *Small Group Research, 16*: 139–156.

Bentley, T. (1994). Facilitation: Providing opportunities for learning. *Journal of European Industrial Training, 18*: 8-22.

Boal, A. (1995). *The rainbow of desire: The Boal method of theatre and therapy*. London, UK: Routledge.

Facilitate. (n.d.). *Dictionary.com Unabridged*. Retrieved from http://dictionary.reference.com/browse/facilitate

Heider, J. (1986). *The Tao of leadership*. Lake Worth, FL: Humanics.

Lewin, K., Lippitt, R., & White, R. K. (1939). Patterns of aggressive behavior in experimentally created "social climates." *Journal of Social Psychology, 10*: 271–299.

Madison, D. S. (2005). Critical ethnography: Method, ethics, and performance. Thousand Oaks, CA: Sage.

Olson, C. D. (1986). *A case study analysis of credentialing in small groups*. Unpublished doctoral dissertation, University of Minnesota.

Smith, C. (2000). Effective facilitation. *Manage, 51*: 16–17.

CHAPTER EIGHT:
Applications of Civil Dialogue

S ince its inception in 2004, we have found Civil Dialogue to be useful in a variety of contexts. Originally conceived as an idea to help families with diverse viewpoints carry out
a civil conversation around a dinner table, Civil Dialogue has evolved into a format that
can be used in many places. Although not an exhaustive list, we believe that these applications
provide strong evidence that it is a productive tool for civil communication in multiple contexts.

ENGAGING COMMUNITIES

Perhaps the most wide-ranging application has been as a tool to facilitate community discussion and productive dialogue about issues that matter to members of local communities. People
who live in community often find themselves disagreeing about a variety of issues from local
zoning ordinances which affect them to larger policy matters. For example, if a large retail store
is proposed for a certain neighborhood, there is often disagreement over whether or not it will
be beneficial to the community. Proponents argue their cost savings measures, while opponents
fear it will diminish their community, create low-wage jobs, and devalue their property. Civic
forums where all issues can be weighed and all viewpoints heard is a perfect application of Civil
Dialogue. By placing people in a protected environment to discuss "hot topics" we urge participants to engage others with their viewpoints, as divergent as they may be, to achieve some level
of understanding within the context of civility. Civil Dialogue is a grass roots effort. Instead
of hosting town hall debates for hundreds or thousands of disgruntled citizens, Civil Dialogue
seeks to get to the root of the issues by inviting people with divergent viewpoints to passionately
and respectfully speak *to* each other. We believe that civil communication practices learned in

Civil Dialogue can allow neighbors to dialogue with neighbors, coworkers with coworkers, and family members with family members, even when they hold deeply divided positions on topics.

The use of Civil Dialogue in specific communities has allowed us to examine the role that power plays in civil exchanges. Lozano-Reich and Cloud (2009) caution us to remember that historical expectations of "standards of decorum" have been used to silence and punish marginalized groups. This informs our position that Civil Dialogue is not about decorum and it does *not* ensure a "safe space" for exchange of ideas. It is impossible for us to know if all participants of a Civil Dialogue are experiencing safety. Rather, we move toward the idea that by offering the format to local communities, whose members may feel deeper trust and connection than they do with external groups, we are diminishing power disparities and allowing groups to come together to disagree. One example of this was a Civil Dialogue held at the Salt River Pima-Maricopa Indian Community in Arizona. We were invited to facilitate a dialogue for the tribal youth members regarding a per capita initiative that the community was considering. Attendance was limited to tribal members between the ages of 16 and 21, with limited access by staff and council members. The youth were given a space to express their positions about the impact that the initiative would/might have on their lives. They challenged one another to think about many aspects of the per capita topic and their examples and stories resonated with one another because of their common experiences, age, and community affiliation. Another group that invited Civil Dialogue to into their space was the Anatolia Turkish-American Community Center. Members gathered to watch the 2016 presidential debate and use Civil Dialogue to process their reactions to the candidates and the impact that their political positions might have on the Turkish-American community. In this instance community members were able to begin their dialogue with a mutual understanding that reflected the similarity of their values and beliefs, yet honored the uniqueness of their political opinions and concerns.

Civil Dialogue has been developed to be a lay-friendly, easy-to-stage format that can cross socioeconomic strata to reach deep into neighborhoods to encourage people to speak from where they are and how they perceive issues at the moment. Such dialogue is essential to counter Portelli's (1994) observation that we've gotten too passive, letting pundits speak for us. Communities are stronger when they get involved in the "hot topics" that affect their lives.

ENGAGING POLITICS

Nowhere is Civil Dialogue more appropriate than on a discussion of provocative political issues. Being a grass roots approach, countless participants have urged us to take this format to Washington, where incivility reigns. We have hosted a series of Civil Dialogues around political issues and elections. One successful application was in conjunction with the presidential and vice-presidential debates prior to the 2012 and 2016 U.S. presidential elections. Civil Dialogue events were sponsored by a host of groups: universities and college campuses, libraries, places of worship, and community centers. Typically, we would tune in to the live broadcast of the debate, using a channel with the least amount of filtration with applause meters, galvanic skin responses, tweets, etc., so viewers would be free, for the time being, of being bombarded with the up-to-the-second analysis of pundits and commentators. Immediately following the debate, before any network host could respond or experts consulted, the Civil Dialogue commenced. A brief introduction of the format was provided, and then a statement reflective of the debate, such as "Candidate X won tonight's debate," was presented. People could spout their political philosophy, indicate their favorites, recall statements from the debate all in an effort to gain mutual understanding of how citizens might come to different conclusions based on the performances of the candidates.

What we also found useful was to see if Civil Dialogue actually changed peoples' minds about what occurred during the debate. A brief survey was conducted using cell phone technology prior to the debate and then at the conclusion of the dialogue to determine if the debate and/or the Civil Dialogue had actually altered peoples' viewpoints about their relative support of the candidates (Olson, Genette, Linde, & Butler, 2018). While most debate watchers already ardently supported one candidate or the other, so there was little political change, there was near unanimity about the positive role of Civil Dialogue in the political process. People admitted to enjoying learning why supporters of candidates were adamant and the overall level of understanding about the democratic process was enhanced.

During "off year" election cycles, we have found it useful to host Civil Dialogue events to allow voters an opportunity to talk about local candidates, particularly controversial ones. In Arizona, perhaps the most visible one is former Maricopa County sheriff, Joe Arpaio. Arguably one of the most controversial public figures in Arizona's political history, Sheriff Arpaio was a source of many Civil Dialogues, with participants eager to discuss the merits of his statements and policies and his unique approach to bringing justice to the Phoenix metropolitan area. Ballot referenda, gubernatorial candidates, senators, etc., are all worthy topics of Civil Dialogue within a local area. Often gathering a cross section of voters, we've found that people of all ages tend to have an interest in politics. Even when an audience is fairly apolitical or unknowledgeable about "off year" issues or candidates, Civil Dialogue can serve as a useful civics lesson, working to fulfill the goal of former Supreme Court Justice Sandra Day O'Connor, who has made one of her primary post court issues that of increasing the knowledge of civics of everyday students and citizens.

ENGAGING RELIGION

Even within a community of people who hold similar religious beliefs, riffs often develop in communities of faith. Despite the doctrines that govern various religions, schisms develop, which often cause derision and division among people who hold similar core values. Civil Dialogue is a natural tool to use to confront issues that hold controversy for various believers. One of our first large public Civil Dialogues happened at a large community church whose congregation was divided on the issue of immigration. Various members of the church had wide-ranging opinions on the value and cost of allowing immigration, largely from Mexico, into the border state, Arizona. Core dialogue participants ranged from an immigration rights attorney to a retired federal police officer who took opposite sides of the statement. Each spoke passionately about their personal experiences with immigration. For those in the audience who were only tangentially impacted by the issue, the panelists' insights were key in formulating opinions. While the goal was not to achieve consensus, merely to help church members understand differences and where those differences sprang from, the dialogue helped increase the understanding and create a greater sense of community of all in attendance on the multifaceted issues of immigration.

Similarly, we have conducted Civil Dialogues with faith-based groups with more specific doctrines and interpretations of scripture. A group of Methodists regularly hold dialogues on contemporary issues such as abortion, the sanctuary movement, community policing, etc. These dialogues prove interesting as oftentimes church leaders will spout church doctrine, if not from the position of a chair, as an audience member, articulating, "This is the policy of the Methodist Church!" Often expected to be immediately accepted, it is helpful for all in attendance to see the wide-ranging opinions that often exist within their membership. Another venue has been in an urban Lutheran church that serves a large homeless population. Replete with the problems facing homeless people, their ministry is often challenged by those who are not frequently given voice in society. By hosting Civil Dialogue events and inviting members of the community to talk about important topics such as prison reform, the death penalty, and sexual violence, this church promotes respect and civility for all members of the congregation and worship community. So useful has Civil Dialogue become that the church's minister has become a certified facilitator and regularly sponsors dialogues at church gatherings.

Civil Dialogue was invited to participate at the Mennonite national convention, held under protest in Phoenix due to Arizona's passage of strict immigration laws, considered to be in conflict with the Mennonite belief system. In fact, while the majority of delegates met in Phoenix, a splinter group met concurrently in Florida, causing upheaval in a typically sedate group. In the dialogues conducted, church leaders, delegates (both clergy and lay), in addition to high school and college students who were attending a simultaneous youth conference participated. Dealing with provocative doctrinal issues, leaders were often stunned by the comments and participation of the student members. Likewise, the student members got a newfound sense of importance as their ideas were listened to with the same intent and interest as church leaders. Many remarked that nowhere before had they witnessed such an egalitarian stance where all ideas were given thoughtful consideration and merit. The mere fact that the dialogue brought together such disparate groups from within the same religion indicates the success of the Civil Dialogue format.

No doubt any religious group could apply Civil Dialogue successfully. Given the plethora of issues which typically divide believers, ranging from the wearing of religious garb to marriage equality, organized religion faces a pull to be contemporary in today's society, while true to the traditional teaching of their various religions. Divisions regularly occur among faith-based organizations, both nationally and locally. Perhaps a greater understanding of the issues which divide people of faith, achieved through participation in Civil Dialogue, may help heal some of the divides which often demand great attention and often sway members from the true calling of their faith.

ENGAGING ORGANIZATIONS

Specific civic organizations and even corporations and work groups can find value in the process of Civil Dialogue. Having been exposed to Civil Dialogue, the California Masons were interested in focusing on bringing civility to their organizational chapters. At their statewide convention, we modeled a Civil Dialogue with their members using a topic they suggested which was causing controversy in their membership. With all members sharing the same core beliefs, their interpretations were different as to how the Masonic principles might be universally applied to all their chapters. Masons of all ages participated, with a special encouragement toward younger members. Following the dialogue, a training session was held so Masonic leaders can extend civil communication practices to their local and regional gatherings and use Civil Dialogue as a problem-solving mechanism for their Masonic chapters facing difficulties. Learning to integrate specific Masonic vernacular became a useful tool to help members understand how civility was embedded in their core principles.

Likewise, Civil Dialogue has been used in concert with meetings of League of Women Voters groups, Arizonans for Gun Safety, as well as other organizations that find themselves in crisis or looking for a way to communicate with civility. Our caution for using Civil Dialogue within a business is that often lower members of the hierarchy may be reluctant to honestly express their feelings for fear of repercussion by supervisors who may well be, at least in part, responsible for issues which lead to the controversy in question. Civil Dialogue is not designed to solve problems or achieve outcomes other than modeling civility and fostering honesty when discussing "hot topics." To the extent that egalitarian Civil Dialogues can be successfully and neutrally facilitated, this format may well work to have applications in business organizations as well as civic ones.

ENGAGING PUBLIC SPACES

The beauty and simplicity of Civil Dialogue is that it can be held anywhere there are five chairs and room for an audience. A variety of public spaces have been used to host Civil Dialogues, and the potential is limitless. For example, one venue often used is an art museum. Two examples illustrate. In 2011, the Arizona State University Museum of Art sponsored "It's Not Just Black or White," an interactive art installation that brought together incarcerated men and women, their families, former convicts, correctional officers, artists, researchers, and members of the community to speak honestly about the penal system in Arizona (http://www.asuartmuseum.org/social-studies-projects/5/Gregory-Sale-It-s-not-just-black-and-white/galleries.html). Civil Dialogue participated in this event as a way for attendees of the museum to process their response to the installation. Secondly, in 2014, the same museum featured "Shifting Sands," a video exhibition that examined the personal, political, and geographical landscapes of the Middle East. Participants had the opportunity to view these works of art, and then attend a Civil Dialogue about the role of the United States in the Middle East. Participants in the dialogue ranged from faculty members, natives of the Middle Eastern countries in question, and students and community members interested in Middle Eastern politics. Given the political nature of the art, lively discussion ensued and both participants and audience members were given the opportunity to share their feelings about this long-standing conflict and the ways it affects people's lives today.

Another public space that is calling for new uses is the public library. Given the explosion of new media, libraries as depositories of books and periodicals are finding fewer and fewer users, thus threatening their viability. Libraries are often looking for new ways to bring community members into their spaces and Civil Dialogue offers a successful entrée back into libraries which exist in nearly every local community. We have sponsored several series of Civil Dialogues in local libraries, each on a topic approved by that library, to help bring people back into that public space. In a community known largely for its elderly populate, we discussed issues regarding aging and age discrimination. In an urban area adjacent to a large park that served as a temporary home for many, topics pertaining to homelessness were discussed. Every community, every area of every city or town has issues of controversy which would be better discussed openly through Civil Dialogue. Public discussion fosters mature and responsible behavior and models the very civility our society seeks to achieve.

In churches, museums, universities, parks, auditoriums, community centers, wherever a few empty chairs can be found, Civil Dialogue can occur. It is in the spaces where we already live, work, and play that people can learn to communicate in civil ways. These community spaces already exist; currently it is the mindset of civility that is the missing ingredient.

ENGAGING CLASSROOMS

Critical pedagogy has a long history of calling for dialogue and asking educators to address complex notions of critical consciousness, social transformation, and agency (Boal, 1995; Friere, 2006; Giroux, 2004). Additionally, notions of institutional power, materiality, and oppressive systems complicate the topic and call for educators to be mindful and cognizant of the work they put forth as "critical" and "pedagogical." Much of our work with Civil Dialogue has been focused on classroom contexts with a desire to provide critical pedagogical practices in a variety of classroom contexts. In 2014 The Hugh Downs School of Human Communication at Arizona State University implemented a certificate in civil communication at the undergraduate level to offer specific training in dialogue-based methods of civility, application of critical civil communication skills in public spheres, and civil and productive modes of argumentation. This specialization provides students with the ability to recognize, competently practice, and facilitate the ever-increasing demand for civil discourse in society and workplace organizations. The certificate includes training in the Civil Dialogue format.

Other classes and high school and university courses can benefit from the use of Civil Dialogue. One example is the basic public speaking course. Typically with a group of individuals who are largely strangers all of who possess various levels of communication apprehension or stage fright, Civil Dialogue offers the perfect opportunity for students to gain confidence by conversationally speaking in front of others without all of the class's attention focused solely on them. It also encourages extemporaneous speech, which is a difficult public speaking skill to teach/learn. Civil Dialogue can be used in public speaking classes as an extension of Foss and Griffin's (1995) notion of invitational rhetoric. Students are typically involved in choosing the topic areas for the dialogue, ranging from campus issues (i.e., a tobacco-free campus or a student fee for athletic team support), to national issues of women's rights, euthanasia, or texting while driving. Though students are not given the exact topic or provocative statement in advance, they are told the topic area and can prepare themselves to participate in a certain topic area. Given the level playing field that all students will ultimately participate in a dialogue, students typically enjoy the opportunity to speak, being less self-conscious than giving a stand-alone speech, and inviting them to find out more about the audience to whom they will be speaking for the remainder of the term. Evaluations for such an assignment can be relatively easy, giving credit for solid opening statements and summaries, use of various forms of evidence, and noting any positive or distracting delivery qualities a speaker may have.

A more rigorous critique can be provided, looking at the substance of what participants say when Civil Dialogue is used in an argumentation course. Often, argumentation classes have found ways to incorporate many styles of debate, where students can often leave feeling like a loser, even if they have put in a substantial amount of work into the assignment. Conversely, Civil Dialogue allows students to demonstrate their argumentation skills, ability to make and support cogent argument, and opportunities to find weaknesses in the positions of others. Cast as a discussion rather than a debate removes the element of winning and losing, persuading or failing to persuade. Sometimes offering two opportunities for Civil Dialogue, one near the beginning of the semester (which often has the same benefits as a dialogue held early in a public speaking course) and one at the end can help mark students' progress as successful producers and consumers of argument.

For several years, Civil Dialogue has been taught in a class called "Performance in Social Context" at Arizona State University. Our goal in this course is utilize the Civil Dialogue format as a performative method. Alexander (2006) reminds us that critical performative pedagogy provides the opportunity to view ourselves and others as a "barometer of truth or reality" (p. 256). This reminder that pedagogy and performance are inclusive of dialogue and generative reflections of truth is the foundational component of the use of Civil Dialogue in this class. Students use Civil Dialogue as a way to process and analyze performances that take up controversial topics and challenging issues. The provocative statement is developed from the content of the performance and allows the audience to process their response to the aesthetic messages through dialogue and discussion.

Civil Dialogue has been used in intercultural communication classes to help students understand various differences in cultural beliefs, practices, and the ways they manifest themselves in life causing riffs which preclude effective communication. We have been invited into conflict and negotiation courses to demonstrate the format as a productive way of processing conflict, and gender and communication classes have used Civil Dialogue as a way to talk about the challenging topics of sexual assault, sexist language, transphobia, and misogyny.

Outside of communication courses, Civil Dialogue is a perfect forum for political science classes. For several years, we have been invited into introductory and advanced political science classes where dialogues have occurred on various political philosophies (i.e., capitalism vs. Marxism), as well as on political issues of the day. With a typically politically interested and informed audience, their discussion often becomes rich with a variety of commentary that adds new levels of sophistication to the Civil Dialogue process.

In short, the potential of the application of Civil Dialogue in the classroom is limitless. Observers who are educators in elementary, junior high, and high schools have often suggested that the format is simple enough to be used to discuss issues relevant to that population (school bullying, stereotyping, etc.). Whatever the pedagogical goal, Civil Dialogue offers the opportunity to experiment with lessons in a myriad of subject areas and on a wide range of topics. Trained Civil Dialogue facilitators in the classroom are a necessity to ensure success in the application of the format to classroom contexts. Having a facilitator who is often unknown to the class helps remove any bias from the role of "teacher" and allows the teacher to be an audience/participant in the dialogue.

REFERENCES

Alexander, B. K. (2006). Performance and pedagogy. In S. Madison (Ed.), *Sage handbook of performance studies* (pp. 253–260). Thousand Oaks, CA: Sage.

Boal, A. (1995). *The rainbow of desire: The Boal method of theatre and therapy*. London, UK: Routledge.

Foss, S., & Griffin, C. (1995). Beyond persuasion: A proposal for an invitational rhetoric. *Communication Monographs, 62*(1): 2–18.

Freire, P. (2006). *Pedagogy of the oppressed, 30th anniversary ed.* New York, NY: Continuum.

Giroux, H. (2004). Cultural studies, public pedagogy, and the responsibility of intellectuals. *Communication and Critical/Cultural Studies, 1*: 59–79.

Lozano-Reich, N. M., & Cloud, D. L. (2009). The uncivil tongue: Invitational rhetoric and the problem of inequality. *Western Journal of Communication, 73*: 220–226.

Olson, C. D., Genette, J, Linde, J., & Butler N. (2018) Changing hearts not minds: The use of Civil Dialogue in presidential and vice presidential debates in *Televised Presidential Debates in a Changing media environment*. Hinck, E. (Ed.). New York, NY: Praeger Press.

Portelli, A. (1994). *The text and the voice: Writing, speaking, and democracy in American lit-erature*. New York, NY: Columbia University Press.

APPENDIX A:
Civil Dialogue Placards

PRINT SPECIFICATIONS:

This document contains eight 8.5 x 11 placard mockups (some of which are used more than once):

- Agree Strongly
- Agree (need 2)
- Agree Somewhat
- Neutral
- Undecided
- Disagree Somewhat
- Disagree (need 2)
- Disagree Strongly

Enlarge each mockup to 11 x 17, print on ordinary white paper, color ink, mount on 11 x 17 foam core to create five placards as follows:

1. "Agree Strongly" on one side, "Agree" on the other
2. "Agree Somewhat" on one side, "Agree" on the other
3. "Neutral" on one side, "Undecided" on the other
4. "Disagree Somewhat" on one side, "Disagree" on the other
5. "Disagree Strongly" on one side, "Disagree" on the other

Low budget option: print on 8.5 x 11 sheets on a desktop printer, adhere to a file folder or other stiff backing.

PLACEMENT:

Best placement is on music stands adjusted to maximum height placed behind each of the five chairs (so the placard is still visible when participants are seated). Allow enough room between the chairs and the music stands so the facilitator has the option of moving behind the chairs.

Low budget option: set the placards on the chairs, have the volunteer speakers set them aside when they take their seats.

AGREE
STRONGLY

AGREE

AGREE
SOMEWHAT

NEUTRAL

UNDECIDED

DISAGREE SOMEWHAT

DISAGREE

DISAGREE STRONGLY

APPENDIX B:
Sample Provocative Statements

POLITICAL TOPICS:

Our country would be best served by electing a political outsider as president in 2020.

Current expressions of free speech have become too extreme.

School vouchers will improve educational equality opportunities.

If you seek or hold public office, you forfeit the right to privacy of ordinary citizens.

"More guns equals more safety." (NRA President Wayne LaPierre)

The majority should prevail.

The U.S. Supreme Court should uphold all provisions of Arizona SB 1070.

Based on tonight's debate, the middle class would be better served by Barack Obama.

Citizens of Maricopa Country made the right choice for sheriff.

Congress should let the United States go over the financial cliff.

"President Obama's healthcare plan is an unfolding disaster for the American economy, a budget bursting entitlement, and a dramatic new federal intrusion into our lives." (Mitt Romney)

America is ready to vote for a Mormon for U.S. president.

Obamacare caused the government shutdown.

The Tea Party is harming the Republican Party.

Todd Akin should have resigned his senate candidacy because of his comments about rape.

"These programs were never about terrorism: they're about economic spying, social control, and diplomatic manipulation." (Edward Snowden)

ECONOMIC TOPICS:

Stabilizing uncertain governments abroad is as important as improving U.S. infrastructure at home.

To stabilize the middle class, taxes on the top 1% of Americans should be increased.

It is time for "wealthy Americans to be patriotic and pay more taxes." (Joe Biden)

Raising taxes makes a bad economy much worse.

Charter schools in Arizona should receive the same state funding as traditional K-12 public schools.

People who work past retirement age are stealing jobs from younger generations.

Baby boomers have been economically irresponsible.

Women don't negotiate wages effectively.

MILITARY TOPICS:

It would be a profound mistake to put American boots on the ground in Syria.

SOCIAL TOPICS:

The best place to decide the issue of gay marriage is with the Supreme Court.

When gays and lesbians remain in the closet they harm the LGBTQ movement.

Conservative viewpoints on immigration are not welcome at this assembly.

Marijuana for recreational purposes should be legalized and taxed.

Illegal immigration is harming the Arizona economy.

Obama's deferred action program for undocumented youth is "blatant political amnesty."

"We should boycott Chick-fil-A. These are our consumer dollars and they're part of our voice."
(NY Governor Elliott Spitzer)

Arizona prisons should not be run by for-profit corporations.

Internet privacy is virtually impossible.

Our fears of homeless people are justified.

MORAL TOPICS:

A doctor is ethically obligated to keep people alive.

There are circumstances that warrant the death penalty.

Doctors should work to preserve human life despite the will of the patient.

The sexual double standard for men and women disadvantages women.

Capital punishment is cruel and unusual punishment.

Employers should be allowed to refuse to cover health services because of "moral reasons."

COLLEGE CAMPUS TOPICS:

ASU's tobacco policy is a good idea.

ASU's new tobacco policy is too restrictive.

Having students monitor ASU's tobacco policy is the best way to ensure compliance.

The ASU and Tempe police forces effectively protect members of the ASU community.

Successful applicants for Deferred Action could be eligible to pay tuition as Arizona residents.

Allowing guns on campus is a bad idea.

Allowing guns on college campuses would make us feel safer.

MISCELLANEOUS TOPICS:

The National Communication Association should take an official position on political issues.

Violent video games do not make you a violent criminal.

Employers have the right to sanction workers who speak negatively about their jobs on Facebook.

The Occupy Movement is proving effective.

School resource officers should not be involved in disciplining a student.

Colin Kaepernick is experiencing racial discrimination from the NFL.

Civil Dialogue®
Hot Topics, Cool Heads

AGREE STRONGLY | AGREE SOMEWHAT | NEUTRAL / UNDECIDED | DISAGREE SOMEWHAT | DISAGREE STRONGLY

Date
Civil Dialogue
Title of Civil Dialogue Event
Location

A round of Civil Dialogue
(30-40 minutes)

- The facilitator presents a controversial or provocative statement to be discussed.
- Audience members consider their positions on the topic.
- Five volunteer participants are recruited from the audience to take a position on the statement.
- The facilitator reviews the ground rules of civility.
- The dialogue:
  - Opening statements from the five speakers
  - Dialogue between the five speakers
  - Audience comments and questions
  - Closing statements from the five speakers
- The facilitator summarizes the round.

About the Institute for Civil Dialogue

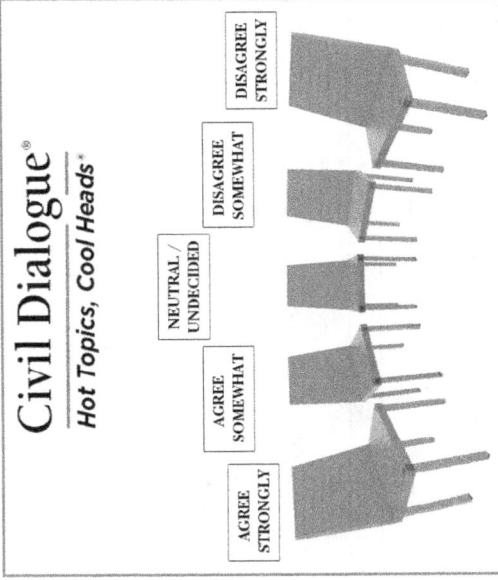

ICD produces events featuring Civil Dialogue, a unique format first developed in 2004 to foster civil spaces for productive dialogue. Diverse positions and identities are welcome and the goal is to acknowledge and understand differences, not necessarily to achieve agreement or consensus.

For more information, visit www.civil-dialogue.com
John Genette: johng@instituteforcivildialogue.org
Jennifer Linde: jlinde @asu.edu
Clark Olson: clark.olson@asu.edu

The Ground Rules of Civility

The goal is productive and civil communication
✓ Be passionate, but not hostile.
✓ Focus on how the statement makes you feel.
✓ Avoid framing the dialogue as an argument.

Participants should use truthful speech that does not attack others.
✓ "I" language shows conviction, "You" language implies critique.
✓ Use your own words and avoid slogans that advocate your position.
✓ Disagree without demonizing.

Participants should use dialogic and reflexive listening practices.
✓ Listen to create successful dialogue and genuine communication.
✓ Listen patiently; do not interrupt.
✓ Do not engage in fake listening as you plan out what you want to say next.

Institute for Civil Dialogue

CD

Civil Dialogue Tracking Sheet – Round 1

Quotation/statement to be discussed:

_____

My position:

Agree (Strongly)	Agree (Somewhat)	Neutral Undecided	Disagree (Somewhat)	Disagree (Strongly)

Why: _____

_____

Names of volunteer speakers:

Agree (Strongly)	Agree (Somewhat)	Neutral Undecided	Disagree (Somewhat)	Disagree (Strongly)

Notes: _____

_____

_____

_____

My critique of the round:

How I feel about the quote now:

Agree (Strongly)	Agree (Somewhat)	Neutral Undecided	Disagree (Somewhat)	Disagree (Strongly)

Why: _____

_____

Civil Dialogue Tracking Sheet – Round 1

Quotation/statement to be discussed:

_____

My position:

Agree (Strongly)	Agree (Somewhat)	Neutral Undecided	Disagree (Somewhat)	Disagree (Strongly)

Why: _____

_____

Names of volunteer speakers:

Agree (Strongly)	Agree (Somewhat)	Neutral Undecided	Disagree (Somewhat)	Disagree (Strongly)

Notes: _____

_____

_____

_____

My critique of the round:

How I feel about the quote now:

Agree (Strongly)	Agree (Somewhat)	Neutral Undecided	Disagree (Somewhat)	Disagree (Strongly)

Why: _____

_____

HOT TOPICS, COOL HEADS: A Handbook for Civil Dialogue

APPENDIX D:
Sample Civil Dialogue Host Introduction

Tempe, Arizona, 2011

Topic: Immigration

Good evening and welcome to Civil Dialogue, where our goal is to invite you to speak and listen to others on challenging topics that typically generate strong responses. We encourage robust and passionate dialogue from our participants—always within an environment of civility.

In recent years the United States has increasingly experienced polarity in public opinion, and more *importantly*, public expression of these opinions. Politicians, competing talkshow hosts, bloggers, and angry tweeters are sharing their perspectives in a variety of mediums, while everyday citizens often remain silent. Recently, the state of Arizona has experienced deep ideological divisions on the topic of immigration that have made it nearly impossible for people living here together to speak to one another civilly.

We believe that people **can** speak to one another. We believe that people who disagree about "hot topics," like immigration policies and laws, can come together in dialogue with "cool heads."

We believe that we can disagree without demonizing.

Civil disagreement is truly possible and people who engage in civil speech and civil listening are helping **all of us** become more informed members of society. Civil speech happens when a person expresses his or her beliefs and values in a passionate yet responsible and truthful manner. Civil listening happens when you attempt to understand a speaker's ideas, feelings, and experiences by listening to him or her with patience and respect.

Let me explain how a Civil Dialogue works. In a moment, I will introduce you to tonight's Civil Dialogue facilitator who will reveal a statement for you to consider. You will note that there are five chairs in our Civil Dialogue semicircle. On a voluntary basis the facilitator will ask you to occupy a chair based on your response to a statement. You may find that you "strongly agree" or just "agree" with the statement. You may "agree somewhat" with the statement, be "undecided" or "neutral" about the statement, or "disagree somewhat," "disagree," or "strongly disagree." After our volunteers are in place, the facilitator will ask each participant to offer a short, 1-minute explanation of why they have occupied that particular chair. After hearing from everyone, the group of five will be invited to participate in an open civil dialogue. This core dialogue will require that participants remain passionate and open-minded while speaking and listening from their chosen position. At the end of 10 minutes, the discussion will be opened to the broader audience for their questions and comments, and then we will return to each member of the core dialogue so that they can offer a brief closing summary of their thoughts.

We have a person who will be our information source on the computer in case we encounter a question that cannot be answered or if there is a potential misstatement of a fact. And, please remember that "facts" are not always easily understood nor as important as they seem. *Your* "fact" may be another person's "opinion." This is _____.

Our facilitator for our first Civil Dialogue is _____.

APPENDIX E:
Sample Civil Dialogue Facilitator Opening Statement

GUNS ON CAMPUS

During this last summer, both the Texas legislature and Texas Governor Greg Abbott signed Senate Bill 11 into law. Specifically, this bill would allow for the carrying of firearms in public buildings on college campuses in Texas. A concern for firearms use on campuses has been sparked by a string of shootings on college campuses, including Northern Arizona University, Umpqua Community College in Oregon, and Texas Southern University. In total, there have been 23 shootings on college campuses to date in 2015, with 13 victims killed and 21 injured across all shootings. Gun rights, let alone laws regulating the carrying of guns on places such as college campuses, carry significant points from both proponents and opponents.

Proponents

Senate Bill 11 is slated to go into effect August 1st, 2016, and is receiving praise for two key points. Texas Representative Allen Fletcher asserted that the bill was filed to protect the rights of people with concealed handgun licenses (CHL) and to permit to "protect themselves in situations where the only two people involved are a law-abiding citizen & a criminal intent on doing them harm—a much more likely scenario than a mass-shooting event." Additionally, the organization, Students for Concealed Carry, praised the passing of this legislation, stating that even though school administrators have the right to enforce and carry out this legislation, this does away with the broad blanket prohibition of firearms on college campuses.

As far as current firearms policies in Arizona schools go, firearms are prohibited on campus with the exception of "any firearm that is lawfully stored and locked in a personally owned motor vehicle or compartment of a motorcycle and not visible from outside the motor vehicle," according to the ASU Police Department Manual. Efforts to pass a bill for guns on campus in Arizona were bolstered and attempted in 2011 after the shooting of former Arizona Representative Gabrielle Giffords, and earlier this year during the first regular session of the Arizona legislature.

Opponents

While there is praise for the signing of Senate Bill 11 in Texas, others are concerned over the impact and danger that guns pose on college campuses. William McRaven, chancellor for the University of Texas system and a former Navy SEALS admiral, was less pleased with the passing of this legislation. In an interview with CNN, McRaven stated, "I've spent my whole life around guns. I grew up in Texas hunting. I spent 37 years in the military. I like guns, but I just don't think having them on campus is the right place."

Additionally, community members at the University of Texas have voiced their concerns over the implementation of this law. According to CNN, over 280 professors have signed a petition calling for a repeal of the law by Texas Governor Greg Abbott. Concerns for campus carry laws have been lingering in the state of Arizona since 2011. Back in 2011 when efforts to pass SB 1467 (a campus carry law), 70% of Arizonans and 56% of gun owners were not looking to expand gun rights on campuses. ASU President Michael Crow has also been consistently adamant about forbidding guns on campus. In a statement made in 2012 during the attempt to pass SB 1474 in Arizona, Crow stated: "I don't oppose gun ownership. Own all the guns you want, I would say to anyone. But please leave them in your car if you bring them to school, which is our present policy.

"ASU Police, the Phoenix SWAT and all the other professional law enforcement chiefs we have talked to are opposed to this bill and say that it will reduce safety. There are places where guns are not conducive to public safety. Schools surely must be on that list."

There are clearly strong opinions on both sides of the topic and I imagine you have strong opinions too. So, now we'd like to invite you to join us in a dialogue to explore the following statement:

ALLOWING GUNS ON COLLEGE CAMPUSES WOULD MAKE US FEEL SAFER.

Please take a moment and write this statement down in your program. While you consider this statement, I'd like to remind you of some ground rules of Civil Dialogue that we ask participants to follow:

First, we encourage you to speak with passion.

Your goal here is not to persuade. So, as you speak with passion be mindful of doing so without forcing your opinions on another.

Engage in dialogue with an open mind; listen carefully. What might you discover that you did not know before?

Lastly, hold to your conviction… but do not demonize someone who doesn't share the same.

Strongly Agree: There is an absolute need to let students and faculty choose how and when to protect themselves when the time comes for such a moment.

Agree: With careful oversight and implementation, it is possible to provide a clear method for campus communities to protect themselves.

Neutral: Campus carry laws are important for student/faculty safety, but there are some concerns that should be thoroughly addressed.

Disagree: The possibility of a campus carry policy is important, but universities may not be able to implement the law in a consistent and safe manner.

Strongly Disagree: There is far too much risk in allow members of any campus community to bear the responsibility of a firearm in a place of learning.

OK. Does anyone see a chair they'd like to take?

Remember if you're uncertain about your position, you can always choose to simply agree or disagree as opposed to strongly agree or strongly disagree, as well as choose to be neutral/undecided. This is YOUR dialogue.

APPENDIX F: Sample Civil Dialogue Facilitator Tracking Sheet

Civil Dialogue— Facilitator Tracking Sheet

Date: _____   Event: _____

Statement/Quotation:

Review of Rules:

The goal is productive and civil communication

Participants should use truthful speech that does not attack others.

Participants should use dialogic and reflexive listening practices.

Timeline (approx. 30–40 minutes):

Intro (first round only) — how CD works, ground rules (5 min.)
Open the round — introduce statement, recruit speakers (5 min.)
Opening statements (5 min.)
Open dialogue (10 min.)
Audience participation (5 min.)
Closing statements (5 min.)
Facilitator summation, close the round (5 min.)

Agree Strongly (name)	Agree Somewhat (name)	Neutral/Undecided (name)	Disagree Somewhat (name)	Disagree Strongly (name)

Audience comments:

Facilitator summation:

111

www.ingramcontent.com/pod-product-compliance
Lightning Source LLC
Chambersburg PA
CBHW080426270326
41929CB00018B/3179